THE BEER DRINKER'S COMPANION

Facts, Fables and Folklore from the World of Beer

John Dallas and Charles McMaster

THE BEER DRINKER'S COMPANION

John Dallas and Charles McMaster

First published in the United Kingdom by The Edinburgh Publishing Company Limited, Admiral House, 30 Maritime Street, Leith, Scotland EH6 6SE

Copyright © 1993 Copyright John Dallas and Charles McMaster

All rights reserved. No part of the contents or illustrative material of this publication may be reproduced, stored in a retrieval system or transmitted in any form or be any means, electronic, mechanical, photocopying, recording or otherwise without the permission of the copyright holder and the Publisher.

British Library Cataloguing-in-Publication Data.
A catalogue record for this book is available from the British Library.

ISBN 1 872401 14 5

Cover illustration: The Public Bar by John Henry Henshaw by courtesy of The Bridgeman Art Library, London.

Printed and bound in the United Kingdom by W. & G. Baird

ABOUT THE AUTHORS

John Dallas, M.A. (Hons)., Dip. Lib.

Born in Edinburgh in 1946 John Dallas is married with two children. He worked in architecture and bookselling before studying history at the University of Edinburgh, where he gained an Honours Degree. He then went on to Wales for a Postgraduate Diploma in Librarianship, after which he worked for the BBC Film Library in London and then Edinburgh University Library. Editor and publisher of the Edinburgh History Magazine, he now mixes freelance work with a part-time post at the Scottish Record Office.

Charles McMaster, B.A. (Hons)

Charles McMaster is one of Britain's leading brewing historians. Educated at Newbattle Abbey College and Strathclyde University, where he achieved an Honours Degree in History, Charles McMaster was the leading light of the erstwhile Scottish Brewing Archive throughout the ten years of its existence in Edinburgh. Now pursuing a freelance career, he is the author of several books on brewing, and has contributed to a wide range of specialist publications. A member of the prestigious British Guild of Beer Writers and the Brewery History Society, he writes and lectures extensively on the history of brewing.

CONTENTS

Acknowledgements, 6

Introduction, 7

What is beer?, 8

Potent porter, 11

Brews and concoctions, 13

The three "Bs", 15

Mother's ruin, 17

Dr. Jekyll's downfall, 19

Imperial beer, 21

Egyptian brewing, 23

The Toucan image, 25

The Yanks and keg beer, 27

The Bear Gates, 31

Bizarre booze, 33

The penurious Pattisons, 35

Lively lager, 37

Saintly sponsors, 43

The Burton brew, 47

Personable pubs and inviting inns, 53

Real ale... really real?, 65

Meted measures, 73

Bottled ale, 75

Edinburgh ales, 77

Befuddled brewing, 81

Tortuous transport, 87

Vigorous Victorians, 93

Highland heather, 105,

Davy Jones brewery, 109

Ablutionary ale, 113

Cans, casks and kegs, 115

Flemish flavours, 119

Some celebratory songs, 123

Glossary of terms, 125

Index, 127

ACKNOWLEDGEMENTS

We would like to acknowledge, in no special order, the help and assistance of all those who have given us their support in the production of this book, particularly Susan Taylor and James Prior of Scottish & Newcastle plc.; Hugh Curley, Michael Theakston, John Griffiths and Jenny Thirsk of T. & R. Theakston Ltd; James Lawrie, Ralph Averbuch, Andrew Reid, Douglas Smith, Peter Moynihan, Ian Whyte, George Insill and John Harrison, each one an expert in his field.

A special thanks is also due to Richard Musson of Scottish & Newcastle plc., a company whose long history of involvement in brewing has produced the inspiration for much of which can be found in the pages of this book, and last but not least warm thanks to Mike Fluskey of The Edinburgh Publishing Company whose patience and professionalism made it all possible.

INTRODUCTION

When we were invited by The Edinburgh Publishing Company to contribute to a series of books, which already included authors of the stature of John Lamond and Ross Leckie, we were pleased to take up the challenge. It not only gave us the opportunity to explore some of the lesser known, but hopefully fascinating, aspects of the history of brewing, but also to explore some of the lesser known, but fascinating, brews along the way.

Throughout history alehouses have provided people from all walks of life with places to relax, to meet friends, to do business, to celebrate, and to generally recharge batteries to face the world. They have been very much at the centre of social life for hundreds of years. Indeed Britain is one of the greatest brewing nations in the world, if not the greatest, and beer has always been our oldest and most traditional drink, from the Leann Fraoch of the Celts and the ale brewed by the monks of the Middle Ages to the great days of the 19th century when British beer was famous throughout the world. The basic techniques of brewing have changed surprisingly little through the ages, but beer itself has many weird and wonderful tales to tell. We have attempted to brew a variety of ways of looking at it from its very beginnings in the Land of the Pharaohs down to developments in more recent times, including the rise of CAMRA and the fall and rise of traditional cask beer.

We hope that those who peruse the book will find it as much fun to read as it was to write. Research has taken us all over the United Kingdom, and even further afield, and this has been a welcome experience, as we have made many friends, and enjoyed many a refreshment with them in the process. You may find, that, like the writing of the book, the reading will prove all the more enjoyable when done with a glass of the magic brew at hand.

John Dallas, Charles McMaster,
Edinburgh Brewing Heritage

WHAT IS BEER?

Although beer is one of Britain's best known and most popular drinks, and has been produced in much the same way since time immemorial, unlike whisky it has in fact no strict legal definition in Britain. Most people assume they know what beer is, but in the United Kingdom there has never been the equivalent of the German "Reinheitsgebot", the Pure Beer Laws first enacted in Bavaria in 1516 and later extended to the entire German Confederation. Norway and Switzerland have similar laws, and, closer to home, even the Isle of Man has its own long-established Pure Beer Law.

The nearest to a definition to be found in Britain is the 1952 Customs & Excise Act which forms the basis for revenue collection on beer. This simply describes beer as anything sold as such which has an alcoholic content in excess of 1% A.B.V. (Alcohol by Volume) and which is made from a wort with an original gravity of in excess of 1016°. Given that this is an attempt by the Exchequer to spread the tax net as widely as possible, this hardly amounts to a strict definition, as there is no mention of permitted raw materials or other ingredients.

Whereas the German laws strictly stipulate water, malt, yeast and hops only (the Manx Laws add sugar to the list), the absence of any such regulations in Britain has led to the widespread use of adjuncts in the mash tun, all-malt brews now being something of a rarity in the U.K. This has in the past debarred British beers from several important continental markets, although now the whole issue of a definition for beer is under review by the European Commission, and it is likely that they will plump for a wider interpretation than Germany to accommodate as many as possible of the member states.

Traditionally, barley has been a major cereal crop in Britain, and this, coupled with cheap barley imports from the Empire and the colonies, enabled British brewers to produce all-malt brews, i.e. those brewed from 100% malted barley. The malting process, however, is very costly with malt being roughly twice the price of raw barley in spite of modern automated malting techniques which have greatly cut down on labour costs.

WHAT IS BEER?

Hence, in the absence of any statutory requirements with regard to raw materials, and given the lack of any strict definition of beer, the way has been open for British brewers, especially in the accountancy-led 1960s and 70s, to substitute a proportion of cheaper unmalted grain in the mash tun. These 'adjuncts', as they are known in the brewing industry, include ingredients such as flaked maize, gries, and rice. A small degree of substitution can in some circumstances actually improve beer quality by eliminating some of the problems caused by all-malt brews - beer haze and excessive yeast reproduction to name just two. The trend, however, has been for up to 30% adjuncts, the loss of extract from the malts being made up by the addition of enzymes.

Accordingly, beer in British terms amounts to little more than a generic and rather nebulous concept, covering a variety of by-product types - ales, stouts, and lagers - produced from a variety of materials. There are no statutory requirements, for example, covering the use of such materials as hops in British beer.

The situation, however, has probably contributed to the wide diversity of the British product for well into the present century many of the larger brewing concerns produced a staggering range of beers:

Table Beers, Breakfast, Luncheon and Dinner Ales, Harvest and Summer Ales, Brown, Double Brown, Oatmeal, Imperial and Invalid Stouts, Old Ales, Strong Ales and Barley Wines, Sparkling Ales, Pale Ales and India Pale Ales (I.P.A.s), Light Ales, Mild Ales, Bitter Ales and Nut Brown Ales, Porter and Milk Stouts, and Export Ales to name but a few.

Although the range shrank considerably after the Second World War, due to the effects of war-time and post-war restrictions and contractions in the industry, some of these beer styles are now making a welcome re-appearance. The export markets for British beers are also witnessing a resurgence, and despite its lack of legal status, British beer seems to be taking a pride in itself once again after the locust years of the 1960s. Britain was once as famous for its beers as anything else, and if they put their minds and skills to it, British beers can still be a world force to be recognised.

A quart of ale is a dish for a king.
- Shakespeare, *A Winter's Tale*, Act. IV. Sc.2

The New Inn, Gloucester

ON THIS DAY IN JANUARY...

1st January 1900
- Edinburgh home to thirty-six breweries.

1st January 1993
- Edinburgh home to two breweries.

Handsel Monday (The first Monday after New Year's Day)
- Sir John Sinclair's "Statistical Account" records the miraculous case of a collier, named Hunter, who loses all use of his limbs and is bedridden for a year and a half with chronic rheumatism. On Handsel Monday visiting friends treat him to quantities of new ale whereby he becomes much intoxicated. On awakening the next day, however, he finds that he is able to get up and walk about. He lives over twenty years after this and never has the smallest return of his illness.

PORTER - THE *ENTIRE* BREW

Porter could claim to be Britain's first national drink. Previously beers differed a good deal from locality to locality, using strictly local practices to produce many distinctive local brews. A popular early 18th century drink, in London in particular, was a mixture of existing brown, strong and old ales. In 1722, however, the Shoreditch brewers Ralph Harwood produced a single brew which embodied the characteristics of the previous mixture. Harwood called the beer "Entire" but as it rapidly became popular with market porters in the East End of London, it soon became known simply as "Porter".

This dark bittersweet beer achieved immediate popularity. The secret of the success was that it was cheap to produce, and could be sold at a lower price than ale, and it could be brewed in bulk, and kept better in the long hot summers.

Porter rapidly spread from the original confines of London, and soon became popular almost everywhere, especially with the burgeoning industrial work force of the Industrial Revolution. Initially demand was met by shipments from London as the intricacies of porter brewing was a closely guarded secret, but this soon leaked out, and porter was produced throughout the land.

In London in 1814, a large storage vat containing 3,500 barrels of porter split open at Meux's brewery. The Resultant flood swept away three houses and drowned eight people.

PORTER - BEER WITH BODY!

Scotsman William Black recounts an alarming tale in his book *A Practical Treatise on Brewing* published in 1835:

"A Dutch house was at that time in the practice of getting whole gyles of Porter brewed for them by one of the great houses in London. On one occasion, one of their clerks was in London at the time of brewing and went to see the process. He, unfortunately, poor fellow, tumbled into a copper of boiling wort and before he could be got out again was actually boiled to death. There were no domed coppers in those days. The gyle of beer was sent over to Holland, and turned out to be very good. The next batch sent, however, did not turn out so well as it had not the same flavour as the preceding gyle. The answer returned by the London house was that they had no means of giving them precisely the same flavour, unless they would send them over another Dutchman..."

THE IRISH TAKE-OVER

The soft water in Ireland proved very successful for porter brewing. Guinness in Dublin developed a stronger form of the beer and christened it "Extra Stout". Gradually this drink took over from porter which lost its cost advantages over other beers and virtually disappeared by the First World War. Today, however, there is a move back to specialist beers, and several breweries are now producing a porter for the first time in many years.

"Beer Street"

What two ideas are more inseparable than beer and Britannia? What event more awfully important to an English colony than the erection of its first brewhouse?

- Sidney Smith, 1771-1845, English writer and clergyman.

Courtyard of the New Inn, Gloucester

ON THIS DAY IN JANUARY...

1st January 1661
- Samuel Pepys records in his diary - "I had for them a barrel of oysters, a dish of neat's tongues and a dish of anchovies, wine of all sorts and a Northdown Ale".

4th January 1916
- Pattisons Ltd. goes into liquidation and with it two of the most colourful characters in brewing history.

4th January 1667
- Samuel Pepys records in his diary - "At night to sup, and then to cards, and last of all to have a flagon of ale and apples, drank out of a wood cup, as a Christmas draught, which made all merry".

BREWS AND CONCOCTIONS

A PINT OF LAMB'S WOOL!

Few enthusiasts today would welcome warm beer but in past centuries hot brews were popular. The wealthy Anglo-Saxons favoured mingling their ale with nutmeg, ginger, sugar, and crab-apples roasted till they burst in white, frothy balls. "Lamb's Wool", as the mixture was called, was carried into the banqueting hall in a huge decorated bowl. When the head of the family drank his share those at the table would cry three times, "Wassail! Wassail! Wassail!" (from Wes hal! - Be Healthy!).

The 17th century English poet Robert Herrick described the ancient rite of "Wassail"-

> Next crown the bowl full
> With gentle Lamb's Wool
> Add sugar, nutmeg, and ginger,
> With store of Ale, too,
> And thus ye must doe
> To make the Wassail a swinger."

BEER FLIP

In the 18th century students warmed up the cold winter nights with "Beer-flip". Beaten egg yolks were added to boiled ale and various flavourings added - sugar, cinnamon, lemon juice etc. - with great care taken over the correct measures and ingredients.

"Aleberry" was ale boiled with sugar and spice with pieces of bread floating on the top.

ALE SYLLABUB - "TAKE ONE COW"

In the 16th and 17th centuries Ale Syllabub was a popular drink in public parks and places which had enough green field for the necessary cow.

One recipe directs "Place in a large bowl a quart of strong ale or beer, grate into it a little nutmeg, and sweeten with sugar. Milk the cow rapidly into the bowl, forcing the milk as strongly as possible into the ale, and against the sides of the vessel, to raise a good froth. Let it stand for an hour and it will then be fit for use."

ALE - THE BUILDING MATERIAL OF THE CHURCH

Ale has, very wisely, never been put to much use other than drinking. In the Middle Ages, however, they did discover one property which now seems forgotten, that of mortar for building. It was believed that mortar mixed with strong ale was much more durable. Many old church accounts show such entries, particularly for the pointing of the church's steeple.

"Tam O'Shanter", Geikie's Etchings

The rapturous, wild, and ineffable pleasure
Of drinking at somebody else's expense.
       - H. S. Leigh, 1837-1883, English author.

*The George Inn,
Norton St. Philip*

ON THIS DAY IN JANUARY...

5th January 1937
- Captain George Ramsden, Chairman of the Halifax brewing firm of Thomas Ramsden & Sons, leaves in his will "a 36 gallon barrel of good ale" for consumption by anyone who attends his funeral.

10th January 1916
- State Management Districts come into being by way of compulsory purchase of all breweries and licensed properties.

10th January 1935
- Beer in cans is first sold to the public in Richmond, Virginia, USA by the Kreuger Brewing Co. of New Jersey.

THE THREE "Bs" 15

BREAD, BEEF AND BEER

In England from the middle ages onwards the staple diet was considered to be that of the three "Bs" - Bread, Beef and Beer.

From the lowest in society to the university halls, ale was the country's number one beverage. In 1617 John Shurle had a job many would envy, that of Ale-taster to Oxford University. He was required to call on every ale-brewer on the day that they brewed in order to taste their ale. For this arduous task he was paid his ancient fee of "one gallon of strong ale, and two gallons of small wort".

When he arrived in London in 1724 the great American statesman and scientist Benjamin Franklin was amazed at the English liking for ale. He worked in a printing office for eighteen months where he noted, "the other workmen, near fifty in number, were great drinkers of beer. We had an alehouse boy, who always attended in the house to supply the workmen. My companion at the press drank every day a pint before breakfast, a pint at breakfast with his bread and cheese, a pint between breakfast and dinner, a pint at dinner, a pint in the afternoon about six o'clock, and another when he had done with his day's work."

A Perfite Platform of a Hoppe Garden.

Training the Hoppe.

"It shalle not be amisse nowe and then to passe through your Garden, having in eche hande a forked wande, directyng aright such Hoppes as declyne from the Poales."

Gathering the Hoppe.

"Cutte them" (the hop stalkes) "asunder wyth a sharpe hooke, and wyth a forked staffe take them from the Poales."

From a pamphlet published in 1574

What contemptible scoundrel stole the cork from my lunch?

- W. C. Fields.

ON THIS DAY IN JANUARY... *The George Inn, Salisbury*

19th January 1736
- James Watt is born at Greenock in Scotland. In 1785 Whitbread install the first steam engine constructed for a "common brewhouse" at the famous old Chiswell Street Brewery. The 35 horse power engine remains in use until sold, still working, to a museum in 1887.

21st January 1949
- Derailment of the train known as "The Newcastle Beer" at Woll, north of Hexham.

29th January 1642
- The "Virgins of the City of London" present a complaint against the continuing civil war demanding the return of "the lusty young men... and handsome journeymen, with whom we had used to walk to Islington and Pimlico to eat Cakes and drink Christian Ale on holy days".

MOTHER'S RUIN

GOOD OLDE ALE VERSUS "MOTHER'S RUIN"

During the 18th century, mainly because of its low price, gin had become an increasingly popular drink among the lower classes. Many of the social problems of the time were blamed on what was called "mother's ruin". There was a continual cry to return to the good "olde English tradition" of ale drinking.

Henry Fielding, magistrate as well as novelist, wrote a treatise blaming the evils of gin as "the parent of crime". William Hogarth, famous for his engravings of social commentary, depicted the contrast between the evils of the one against the virtues of the other in his two engravings *Gin Lane* and *Beer Street*. While buildings are derelict, mothers are drunk, children are neglected and riots abound in the Lane, in *Beer Street* all is happiness and plentiful as businesses thrive, new buildings go up and even the French are vanquished. The message was plain and simple "Beer is best" (and patriotic) and the government moved to remedy the situation.

The Beer Act of 1830 was a major attempt to re-establish beer as the national drink. The Act allowed any rate-paying householder the right, on the payment of two guineas excise, to sell beer without a licence. Within a few months nearly 25,000 people had set themselves up in their "alehouses". In the first few weeks of the Act in Liverpool alone fifty new beer shops were opened every day. The Act, however, only increased the social problems. By the 1850s the number of beer-shops had multiplied to such an extent that small shop-keepers and householders had set themselves up in any spare room, hallway, cellar or shed they could find.

Further legislation was obviously needed; 1834 saw the introduction of "off licences"; 1869 brought beer-houses under magisterial control; 1872 licensing hours were introduced. All of which are still the basis for providing respectable venues in which the beer lover can enjoy his national drink.

"Gin Lane"

Prohibition makes you want to cry into your beer, and denies you the beer to cry into.
                    - Don Marquis, 1878-1937,
                       American journalist.

ON THIS DAY IN JAN/FEB...   The George Inn, Salisbury, 1858

1st February 1686
- The government encourages magistrates to issue as many licenses as they could as "The more Ale Houses there are the better it is for the Excise".

3rd February 1761
- *The London Gazette* reports tumults in Norwich and threats of "popular action" against the London brewers at the rise in beer prices to 3 d. a pot. They had been at 3d. a pot for nearly 40 years.

9th February 1804
- Truman's Brewery refuses to accept responsibility for their Porter when sent on long voyages. Writing to one of their customers they state "it is impossible to guard against the causes of Porter losing its quality, in cask, on a voyage to the West Indies" and that they "did not hold themselves liable to any loss that may arise".

BLACK CORK - THE REAL "DR. JEKYLL'S" DOWNFALL!

It is well known that Robert Louis Stevenson used the story of Edinburgh's notorious Deacon, William Brodie, as the inspiration for the terrible tale of *Dr. Jekyll and Mr. Hyde*.

The two had much in common. Deacon Brodie was by day a prominent and respectable Edinburgh citizen, A Deacon of the Incorporation of Wrights (cabinet-makers), and a pillar of the Edinburgh community. By night, however, he led a very different life as a thief and house-breaker. Throughout much of the 1780s he carried out a series of audacious robberies in the city, and might well have remained undetected forever.

In August 1788, however, he overreached himself in attempting to rob the Excise office for Scotland. One of the gang was apprehended, Brodie escaped but knew his cover was blown. He fled to Holland where he was later arrested, and sent back to Scotland to stand trial. What is so not well known is that the infamous Deacon like his fictitious counterpart also partook of a "special" brew!

At the trial, one of the accused told how he and Brodie and two others had met in a house belonging to one of the gang. He testified that when preparing for the ill-fated robbery, "they had some herrings, chicken and Black Cork".

"What" asked the judge" is "Black Cork?".

The defendant explained that it was a particularly favoured strong Scotch Ale, otherwise known as "Bell's Beer" after its brewer, Bartholomew Bell. Bell was a noted Edinburgh brewer of the mid 18th century, whose speciality was the production of dark "Scotch" ales of exceptional strength and quality, most notable being the aforementioned "Black Cork". The excellence of Bell's beer was universally recognised.

In 1755 the Edinburgh Society awarded him a prestigious medal in recognition of this, and in 1849 Thomson's book *Brewing and Distillation* stated that Bell's beer "became celebrated not only in Edinburgh, but all over the kingdom, as the very best that the Scotch system of brewing could produce... The method of brewing it was kept secret by the brewers, and when their brewery was given up, production of it ceased". Bell's brewery closed in 1837 and the secret recipe for "Black Cork" died with it.

In October 1788 the original "Dr. Jekyll" was publicly hanged on a gibbet which as Deacon of the Wrights he himself had helped to design. A well known Edinburgh public-house bearing his name overlooks the site where the Deacon met his untimely end, and while it may no longer purvey "Black Cork" it is possible for the curious to sample a small refreshment while pondering the dangers of strong brews.

"Deacon Brodie", Kay's Portraits

I'd hate to be a teetotaller. Imagine getting up in the morning and knowing that's as good as you're going to feel all day.
                    - Dean Martin, born 1917.

The Bell, Hurley

ON THIS DAY IN FEBRUARY...

10th February 1695
- The Anchor Brewery in Southwark exports "15 tunns of XX Beer sent to Beerbadoes - £24".

11th February 1791
- London brewers Robert Barclay and Joseph Delafield reporting on Anglo-Irish trade to the Privy Council state "The export trade from London to Ireland is for the most part Porter, of which London is the principal or chief marker".

12th February 1945
- S.S. Egholm is sunk by a mine on passage from Leith to London with a full cargo of Wm. Youngers' beer.

IMPERIAL BEER

BEER AND EMPIRE

One of the beers with which Britain became closely identified with during the course of the 19th century was I.P.A. or India Pale Ale. Thought to have been originally formulated in the 1780s by the London brewer Richard Hodgson, India Pale Ale was quickly adapted by provincial brewers in centres such as Burton and Edinburgh, where the hard water was eminently suitable for light sparkling beers of this type.

The secret of the success of pale ales was the relatively low gravity married to high hop levels which made it last well over hot summers. The relatively low gravity also made it a popular drink for general consumption at a time when water supplies were still very poor in many towns. During brewing, water-borne diseases such as cholera, typhoid and scrofula were eliminated by the boiling process, and the attraction of a relatively innocuous but safe drink was obvious.

The potential for the export market quickly became apparent. As British imperialist expansion proceeded apace during the 19th century, vast new overseas markets were opened up leading to a greatly increased demand for beer shipments abroad. Previously only the strength of the older style darker British beers had prevented them from turning sour on long sea voyages, but the newer pale ales travelled well and kept their condition and clarity in hot climates. The advent of pasteurisation and carbonation at the turn of the century led to a great expansion in overseas bottled beer exports. The stable beer that resulted could be bottled almost immediately and was little affected by rapid temperature changes.

The military market in the Indian sub-continent was a particularly large and discerning one for British beers, and as a result many breweries began to produce "India Pale", "Export" and "Imperial" beers specifically for this and other colonial markets. Pale Ale became associated in the public mind with the British army regiments serving in the colonies and advertisements featured it as the soldier's drink. As the army's popularity rose during the 1890s, India Pale Ale became a leading brand in the home market.

The retreat from colonialism and the decline in Britain's world role after the Second World War signalled the end for many specialist Export beers. Although domestic variants survived they also seemed to be in decline. The reputation of India Pale Ale persisted, however, and recent years have seen a home market resurgence of "The beer of the Empire".

A CLEAR END TO THE "CLOUDY" PINT

One factor which accelerated the trend away from the older darker ales and porters towards the newer lighter sparkling pale ales was the gradual replacement of earthenware and pewter jugs, bottles and tankards with glassware receptacles. It had mattered little that many of the older drinks were decidedly murky in character as it was impossible to see with the drinking vessels that were available. The removal of the excise duty on glass manufacture in 1895 meant that glass began to replace the older materials for drinking vessels. The clarity of pale ale was there for all to see.

AT LUNCH

we *all* agree that

beer is best

Some men are like musical glasses - to produce their finest tones you must keep them wet.

- S. T. Coleridge, 1772-1834.

ON THIS DAY IN FEBRUARY...

The Bell, Waltham St. Lawrence

14th February 1554
- The old Assembly Books of Great Yarmouth state that, "Feb. 14 I Philip and Mary, 1554. M. Swansey of Hicking, being a foreigner, bought of a merchant stranger certain hopps - the buyer to forfeit the Hopps, and he may buy them again of the Chamberlain".

15th February 1937
- Brewers' yeast is used in sandwiches supplied free to hundreds of under-nourished schoolchildren at Glossop, Derbyshire. Brewers' yeast contains the highly important vitamins, B1 and B2, which accelerate and stimulate growth.

15th February 1798
- An Admiralty Order instructs all issue of essence of malt discontinued. The hopes that beer might be an antidote to scurvy comes to an end after successful use of lemon juice.

EGYPTIAN BREWING

THE BEER OF THE PHARAOHS

Although the brewing of beer is now particularly associated with Britain and Europe it did not originate in either of these areas, but in the Middle East. Ancient wall paintings and tomb models reveal brewing in Mesopotamia and Egypt from around 2,000 years before Christ.

The secret of Egyptian brewing has hitherto been lost in the mists of time but this situation may be about to change with excavations being carried out by the Egypt Exploration Society at the site of the ancient city of Tel-el-Amarna. This was once the most important city in Egypt, home to the palace of Pharaoh Tutankhamen and Queen Nefertiti. Situated 200 miles south of Cairo, the city was the site of a dig by a team of archaeologists from Cambridge University.

Here they discovered clay jars containing grain and other utensils which indicated that it was the site of the legendary Pharaoh's brewery, part of the lost Sun-Temple of Tutankhamen.

In an attempt to understand exactly how the Egyptians brewed their beer, research has been carried out in Britain by archeo-botanists in conjunction with the chemists of a leading brewery company, Scottish and Newcastle Breweries. Boreholes have been drilled on the site in Egypt so analysts can determine the quality of the water involved in the process. It is planned to set up a micro-brewery on the site in order to replicate as closely as possible the conditions under which brewing took place.

From the research already undertaken it would appear that the brewing of beer and the baking of bread were both closely linked. The surplus grain from the baking was combined with whey from the dough and fermented with the addition of dates, herbs such as coriander, and roots. Honey is also thought to have been added. Trial brews are taking place in Britain but, according to the experts, it is unlikely ever to be sold commercially as it will hardly be to the modern taste. Research also indicates that the beer was primarily used as a form of sustenance for the slaves engaged on the building of the pyramids. An added form of punishment, perhaps?

I drink when I have occasion, and sometimes when I have no occasion.

- Cervantes, Don Quixote.

ON THIS DAY IN FEBRUARY...

15th February 1946
- H.M.S. Menestheus arrives at Yokohama on its maiden voyage. The ship has been converted to carry an on-board brewery to supply beer to the British and Allied troops.

20th February 1936
- The Chief Constable of Kendal warns licensed premises in the area that they will have to stop offering free beer, cigars and sandwiches as an enticement to customers.

THE TOUCAN IMAGE

WHEN IRISH EYES WERE SMILING

Think of beer and brewing in Ireland, and you automatically think of stout, that dark bitter and sweet beer with the creamy head. If you are old enough you might also have the image of a Toucan in your head! Irish stout, Guinness, Murphys and Beamish are famous the world over, but the reasons for the Irish dominance in this market are not so well known.

Stout was indeed a stouter or stronger version of Porter, that mysterious 18th century drink which has now largely died out. Porter emigrated to Ireland in the 1750s, the soft water in that country being extremely suitable for beers of this type. There were also many areas on the mainland of Britain which specialised in Stouts and Porters, particularly towns such as London and Glasgow where the water was suitable. Irish products competed on quality terms with the mainland product, but the domestic market in Ireland was small and poor, and much of the total output was shipped to places like Liverpool, Cardiff and Glasgow where there was a big Irish immigrant community.

This situation prevailed until the First World War. Ireland was at that time still part of the United Kingdom, but the relationship had often been stormy, with much political agitation and agrarian unrest in Catholic Ireland. When the Defence of the Realm Act was passed in 1915, imposing stringent restrictions on all manner of activities, including brewing, the terms of the Act were, for reasons of political expediency, not extended to Ireland for fear of further exacerbating the civil unrest which within a year culminated in the Easter Rising. In fact John Redmond, the moderate Irish Nationalist leader stood up in the House of Commons and made an impassioned plea that impoverished unstable Ireland be spared the Defence of the Realm Act. Interestingly, conscription was not extended to Ireland either, all Irish serving soldiers being regulars, territorials or volunteers.

The effect of this decision was to place the mainland brewers at a marked disadvantage, as they laboured under raw material, output and gravity restrictions while facing unfettered competition from their Irish counterparts. With the Irish Sea being protected by boom vessels and submarine nets, the Irish brewers, Guinness, Murphy and Beamish took advantage of the situation by shipping vast amounts of stout to the mainland. Their position was so strengthened over these years that the mainland opposition was decimated. In Glasgow, for example, only a handful of breweries survived the war, and most of those abandoned the unequal struggle and succumbed shortly afterwards. Guinness, despite having no tied estate on the mainland, became a national drink, available in virtually every pub in the country.

Good ale is meat, drink and cloth.
- Old English proverb

The Ostrich, Colnbrook

ON THIS DAY IN FEB/MAR...

1st March 1786
- One of the Whitbread brewers writing to his brother describes how "Last summer we set up a steam engine for the purposes of grinding our malt and raise our liquor... we have put aside now full 24 horses by it, which to keep up and feed cost more than £40 a head per annum. The expenses of erecting the engine was about £1,000".

12th March 1283
- Bristol magistrates warn brewers that if they are found charging more than 1 d. for a gallon of strong ale, or 1d. for light ale, their brewery will be forfeited and the transgressor punished.

THE YANKS AND KEG BEER

HOW THE YANKS AFFECTED OUR BEER

During the Second World War many American servicemen were stationed in Britain. By and large they liked the "Old Country", regarding it as quaint and sometimes amusing. They liked the women too, but were rather more ambivalent about our beer. Traditional British draught beer they regarded as flat, warm and uninteresting but they quite liked our carbonated bottled beer which reminded them more of "What Made Milwaukee Famous" and the beer back home. The trouble was that by the mid-war years there was a bottle shortage in Britain and little bottled beer being produced.

A POINT OF HONOUR

One of the largest American contingents in Britain was the U.S. Air Force. From 1942 onwards they were involved in the daylight bombing war against Germany but this proved a costly effort both in aircraft and manpower. After the disastrous raid against the German ball-bearing factory at Schwienfort in 1943 the losses were devastating and morale understandably low. The U.S.A.A.F. tried to do what they could for the shattered aircrews. In the absence of more tangible benefits, such as long-range escort fighters, the U.S.A.A.F. aimed to ensure that their boys would at least never be short of a beer. As the big four-engined Fortresses and Liberators taxied to a halt after returning from bombing missions, the U.S. Air Force made it a point of honour that their aircrew could have a beer as soon as they alighted from their aircraft at the dispersal points. The trouble was, given the shortage of bottled beer, that if you put a firkin of traditional British beer on the back of a jeep and bumped it over an airfield, it would be virtually undrinkable by the time it reached the aircraft.

METAL CASKS

This problem sorely tried the U.S. Air Force. Many of the biggest American air bases were in East Anglia, and Air Force General Curtis Le May approached big brewers Greens of Luton to see if they could help. Carbonated beer in cask was not entirely unknown, being used for ships stores and the like, but Greens patiently explained that to produce bottle-type carbonated beer in casks was impractical, as the extra pressure would blow out the staves in the wooden barrels. "Why not use metal casks?" enquired the U.S.A.A.F. Bernard Dixon, Head Brewer of Greens explained that the cost of acquiring strengthened casks would be quite prohibitive. "How much?" asked General Le May. When told it would be at least £100,000, an enormous sum of money for those days, he immediately wrote a cheque for exactly that amount.

Metal casks

THE BEER DRINKER'S COMPANION

The flowing bowl - whom has it not made eloquent? Whom has it not made free, even amid pinching poverty?

— Horace, 65-8 B.C.

The George Inn, Ripley

ON THIS DAY IN MARCH...

13th March 1718
- The Commissioners of Excise first complain to the Treasury that "for some time past the brewers have made their common strong beer of greater strength than usual". The practice of brewing extraordinarily concentrated beer has been in effect for defaulting the revenue.

15th March 1830
- The Chancellor of the Exchequer *abolishes* the tax on beer! This stands for fifty years until its re-introduction in 1880.

THE YANKS AND KEG BEER

CARBONATED BEER

The U.S. Air Force's fortunes improved by 1944 with the arrival of the splendid Mustang and Thunderbolt escort fighters. Greens of Luton did very well out of supplying the Americans, enabling them to merge with Flowers of Stratford and Cheltenham. Bernard Dixon was convinced that carbonated bulk beer, a stable product with a long cellar life which could be handled by unskilled bar staff was the way forward in the post-war years, and many other brewers followed suit. Indeed, Dixon set up his own company, Keg Investments Ltd., to pursue the aim of converting breweries to kegging. Raw material restrictions, including the import of high quality malting barleys, were not lifted until the mid 1950s, and this was another argument in favour of pasteurised keg beer for the variable quality of brewing materials available could be ironed out somewhat in the kegging process.

REAL ALE MAKES A COMEBACK

The post-war years also saw a general trend towards *convenience* foodstuffs. Frozen peas, fish fingers, TV dinners, instant mashed potato, all came on the market, and for the brewers and publicans pasteurised keg beer was a *convenience* beer. Trends change, however, and eventually there was a reaction to the quality and content of what was on offer. Convenience took a back seat to taste and quality as the consumer demanded a more natural product. "Real ale" made its comeback.

Whilst it would be wrong to blame the Americans for inflicting the dubious pleasures of keg beer on the British beer drinker, undoubtedly the war in general accelerated the trend. In defence of keg beer it can only be said that there were very sound reasons for its introduction at the time. Fortunately these reasons have now largely lost their relevance.

*Come landlord fill a flowing bowl
until it does run over,
Tonight we will all merry be -
tomorrow we'll get sober.*
　　　　　- John Fletcher, 1579-1625, The
　　　　　　　　Bloody Brother.

ON THIS DAY IN MARCH... 　　　*The King's Head, Chigwell*

20th March 1937
- A constable at Lambeth Police Court produces a quantity of what he calls "Red Biddy" which he has found beside a woman found drunk and incapable. The magistrate dismisses the woman with the advice "That stuff is absolute rat poison. If you had stuck to good, honest beer you would not have ended up here. Go away!".

THE BEAR GATES

THE GATES ARE STILL CLOSED ON BEAR ALE

Traquair House at Innerleithen near Peebles is reputably the oldest continually inhabited house in Scotland, dating back more than 800 years to the time of Alexander 1st of Scotland who signed a charter here in the 12th century. Mary Queen of Scots is known to have visited the house in 1566, and Charles Edward Stuart, the Young Pretender, stayed at Traquair House in 1745 during the course of the Jacobite Rebellion.

Indeed, on his way south to Derby, "Bonnie Prince Charlie" departed from Traquair House by way of the famous Bear Gates, named after the carved stone bears which surmount the gate-posts. The Laird of Traquair, a noted Jacobite supporter, vowed the gates would remain closed until a Stuart was restored to the throne of the United Kingdom. As a consequence, the Bear Gates have remained unopened from that time until the present day.

While staying at Traquair House it is known that Charles Edward Stuart and his entourage partook of the famous ale of Traquair, and the story of Traquair's Brewhouse is as fascinating as that of the house itself. It is thought that ale has been brewed at Traquair since time immemorial, but had ceased well over a century ago. In 1965, however, the 20th Laird of Traquair, the late Peter Maxwell Stuart, was cleaning out some old cellars that had not been used in living memory, when he discovered a complete 18th century brewhouse intact, still with the original oak-lined open brewing copper, mash tun, open coolers and fermenters and wooden stirring paddles. The Laird decided to renovate the brewhouse and put it back into commission using the original vessels, which are thought to date from the 1730s.

This venture proved to be a great success. Whereas formerly the Traquair Brewhouse would have been used to supply the household and the estate workers with ale, an important part of the diet in the 18th and 19th centuries, now it is supplied to the visitors who flock to the House in the summer season, and to specialist beer outlets all over Britain and further afield. The Laird's daughter Catherine still carries on the brewery and annual production is far outstripped by demand. Constrained by size the 320 barrels a year brewed include the famed 1076° gravity Traquair House Ale, a very potent drink, and the less strong but still formidable Bear Ale, named after the Bear Gates, at 1050°. Most of the output is bottled and exported to as far away as the USA, France and Japan.

The revived Traquair House Brewery can be seen as the fore-runner of many of the new small breweries which have sprung up in Britain over the last few decades, and this, coupled with its long and fascinating history, ensures that it is enshrined in the pantheon of British Brewing.

Traquair Bear Gates

If a man has a bit of a conscience, it always takes him when he's sober; and then it makes him low-spirited. A drop of booze just takes that off and makes him happy.
   - George Bernard Shaw, 1856-1950,
                              Pygmalion.

*The Five Gables, Shakespear Hotel,
Stratford-on-Avon*

ON THIS DAY IN MARCH...

25th March 1971
- The State Management Districts are to be returned to the private sector and all assets disposed of.

31st March 1891
- The Inland Revenue Reports reveal the number of barrels of beer brewed in the year 1890-91 to be 31,927,303.

31st March 1961
- Brewing ceases at St. Ann's Brewery in Edinburgh (Robert Youngers).

BIZARRE BOOZE

THE ALE DRAPER!

A common designation for an alehouse-keeper in the 16th century was that of an Ale draper. In *Kind Harts Dreame*, written in 1592, Henry Chettle revealed his ambitions:

"I came up to London, and fall to be some tapster, hostler, or chamberlaine in an inn. Well, I get mee a wife; with her a little money; when we are married, seeke a house we must: no other occupation have I but to be an ale-draper."

EGYPT'S "ABOMINABLE" BOOZER

The following report from Egypt appeared in the *Morning Chronicle* of August 27th 1852:

"I should mention also an abominable mixture which my crew had with them on the river: it was a liquor called 'Boozer', and said to be intoxicating. It is much in vogue among the lower orders in Egypt, and I find that it is made from a fermentation of bread in water. I thought it peculiarly filthy, but it is said to have been used in ancient Egypt, and to be the liquor mentioned by Herodotus."

THE NEED OF EMPIRE

On October 10th 1857 the following plea appeared in a monthly magazine from a correspondent signing himself "A Soldier's Friend":

"Concentrated or portable beer for our soldiers in the East.

Can any of your readers inform me whether it is possible to manufacture such an article as the above, as it would be invaluable to our private soldiers in the East Indies, where such a tonic as beer is absolutely requisite?

In Russia, the soldiers make use of the quass loaves (their small beer), which are made of oat or rye meal with ground malt and hops, made into cakes either with plain water or an infusion of hops. Sometimes the Extract of Malt is added, which is nothing more than sweet wort evaporated to the consistency of treacle. The cakes are then baked and kept for use. Infused for 24 to 30 hours in boiling water, they make a wholesome, nourishing and strengthening drink."

Cornelius Caton, Ale-draper

There are some sluggish men who are improved by drinking.
                - Samuel Johnson, 1709-1784.

The Bell Inn, Tewksbury

ON THIS DAY IN MAR/APR...

1st April 1785
- *The Times* reports "There is a cask now building at Meux & Co.'s brewery in Liquorpond Street, Gray's Inn Lane, the size of which exceeds all credibility being designed to hold 20,000 barrels of Porter". This is the same vat that bursts in 1814 killing eight people.

1st April 1799
- Arthur Guinness, now an old man, records in one of his firm's brewing books the company's historic decision to concentrate on brewing stout and porter stating "Today, April 1st 1799, was brewed the LAST ale brew".

THE RISE AND FALL OF THE HOUSE OF PATTISON

Amongst the most colourful figures to grace the British brewery scene in the late 19th century were the Pattison brothers, Robert and Walter, whose brief burst of fame was matched only by their startling fall from grace in the 1890s. The Pattison brothers originally started out in the licensed trade in Leith in Scotland, before moving into whisky broking and blending, and eventually in 1895, into brewing by building a substantial modern brewery at Duddingston near Edinburgh.

At a time before the advent of any mass media, and when advertising was still relatively restrained, the Pattison brothers were noted for their showmanship and flair for publicity. This coupled with their extravagance caused raised eyebrows in many staid Victorian circles. In order to gain outlets for their products, the Pattisons bought into licensed premises in Scotland and the north of England and also acquired other outlets through loan-ties. This tied house estate gave rise to one of Pattisons most ingenious advertising campaigns, namely the distribution to those public houses selling their products, and to Pattison salesmen, of grey parrots specially trained to squawk the praises of Pattison's ales. Some of their advertising doggerel was pretty dire too, for example:

North, South, East, West
Pattison's Ales are the best,
East, West, North, South,
Pattison's Ales in every mouth

The company seemingly prospered in the late 1890s, enabling both brothers to live in large mansion houses in the most opulent and extravagant style. They also indulged in another of their favourite advertising ploys - the deliberate missing of trains! Both brothers would contrive to miss the early morning business express into Edinburgh, and having alerted the press well in advance, would ostentatiously hire a special train to convey themselves at the cost of 5 guineas per mile. In the short term, it seemed to work very well indeed, and Pattison's Ltd. continued to announce very promising annual figures and pay substantial dividends to their shareholders.

In late 1898 a slump set in and rumours began to circulate that the Company was in financial difficulties. The Pattison brothers had borrowed heavily from the banks over the preceding few years, and were now frantically trying to borrow even more to shore up the business. A meeting of the creditors in January 1899 discovered that the Company was not only hopelessly insolvent, and had been so since it had been floated some years previously, but also that falsified annual accounts had been issued.

The truth was, that to maintain confidence and a spurious solvency, Pattisons had simply been paying dividends out of new subscriptions. This was only feasible while trade continued to expand, but once there was a downturn, the whole edifice began to crumble.

Criminal charges were now brought and in 1901 both brothers were convicted of fraud and sent to prison. The Pattison saga was over.

Pattison's brewery

Then trust me there's nothing like drinking
So pleasant on this side the grave,
It keeps the unhappy from thinking,
and makes e'en the valiant more brave.
  - Charles Dibdin, 1745-1814,
           Nothing like Grog.

Beams in the Porch Room,
George Inn, Salisbury

ON THIS DAY IN APRIL...

9th April 1473
- A lease is drawn up made to one John Gryme, a saddler, and contains a description of the ancient George Inn in Salisbury and an inventory of furniture. The house contains thirteen chambers, viz:- The Principal Chamber, the Earl's Chamber, the Pantry adjoining, the Oxford Chamber, the Abingdon Chamber, the Squire's Chamber, the Lombard's Chamber, the Garret, the George, the Clarendon, the Understent, the Fitzwaryn, and the London Chamber.

LIVELY LAGER

THE LAGER PHENOMENON IN BRITAIN

Although to many drinkers in the British Isles the growth of lager drinking is a fairly recent and puzzling phenomenon, it has in fact a long and respectable pedigree in Britain, stretching back well over a century.

Lager beer - "lager" being the German word for store - first became available in Britain during the third quarter of the 19th century when it began to be imported into this country on a relatively small scale from its homelands in Germany, Denmark and Holland. The reason for its importation was the growing public demand for light sparkling beers of clarity and relatively low gravity, which coincided with the switch away from the older dark beers such as strong ale, porter and stout. These latter beers were often murky in character, which mattered little when earthenware and stone bottles, and pewter tankards were in use, but the gradual move towards glass receptacles was in favour of the clearer drinks. Lager, being in the early days exclusively a bottled beer, was well placed to take advantage of this.

Lager brewing and storage, however, presented the traditional British ale brewers with new problems - specially kilned malts and bottom fermentation processes, the need for strict low-temperature controls, filtration, pasteurisation and long conditioning. With refrigeration still in its infancy, and with lager beers as yet forming a small, if growing sector of the overall market, few brewers felt it worthwhile to go to the expense of installing the necessary equipment, preferring to concentrate instead on top-fermentation pale ales. In spite of these problems, however, lager sales continued to make inroads into the traditional export markets of the British brewers and several of the companies accepted the challenge to produce their own lager.

London, Wrexham and Glasgow have all laid claim to having produced the first British lager, but recent research suggests Edinburgh beat them all to it. William Younger & Co. started brewing lager beer at their Holyrood Brewery in Edinburgh in December 1879 using a yeast strain imported from the Carlsberg Brewery at Copenhagen. Youngers brewed lager for a number of years in the 1880s but in the final event did not persist with the product. New advances in refrigeration meant that much better temperature control could be obtained in the brewing and fermenting of pale ales and Youngers decided to concentrate on this type of beer.

"Very fou", Geikie's Etchings

PREMIUM ORIGINAL
GILLESPIE'S
MALT STOUT
BREWED IN EDINBURGH
SCOTTISH MALT STOUT
GILLESPIE'S

GILLESPIE'S SCOTTISH MALT STOUT

Although most often thought of in recent decades as primarily an Irish product, Stout has in fact a long and fascinating tradition in Scotland, and in particular in Edinburgh, where *Gillespie's Malt Stout* is brewed. Stout is a derivative of that somewhat mysterious 19th century drink Porter, which could reasonably claim to be Britain's first truly national beer style. Porter, a dark-brown sweet but slightly sour drink, was replaced from the mid 19th century onwards by Stout, a stronger and dryer dark beer which thereafter remained the dominant style.

The use of the word 'stout' in its adjectival sense, meaning strong, predated the use of the word as a noun by about a century. Stout was a word often ascribed to any strong brew, and in an 1810 Memorandum Book by a famous Irish brewing company there is mention for the first time of a 'Stouter form of Porter'. Within a few decades most of the beers sold by this Dublin company went under the name of 'Stout'.

In Edinburgh, Porter was brewed since at least 1750, and in 1806, William Younger announced that he was joining forces with his brother Archibald Campbell Younger in a Porter brewing venture. Although Porter became a substantial part of Younger's total output during the first half of the 19th century, by 1875 all had been replaced by Stouts - Single Stout, Brown Stout and Double Brown Stout being pre-eminent. These were later joined by Oatmeal Stouts and Imperial Stouts, the latter being strong export versions of the drink. Stouts did not need the lengthy maturation period demanded by Porter, and were easier to produce.

Stout and Porter brewing were badly hit in mainland Britain during the First World War by restrictions on raw materials, gravities and output, but these restrictions were not extended to Ireland for fear of exacerbating civil unrest there. This enabled the Irish Stout and Porter brewers to get a stronghold on the British market. As a result Scottish stout receded into history.

That is until, in 1992, due to popular demand, the first new draught Scottish Stout to be produced by Scottish & Newcastle plc. for many years was launched under the title of *Gillespie's Malt Stout*, the name in itself commemorating an old Scottish brewery company which was very famous at one time for its stout. This 4% A.B.V. dark Stout is brewed with the addition of black malt and roasted barley giving a classic dark and not too bitter drink with a fine aroma and a creamy head. As well as being available in draught form, *Gillespie's Scottish Malt Stout* is available in 440ml. cans with the revolutionary new **TAPSTREAM SYSTEM**™ recreating the draught presentation.

Gillespie's heralds a welcome return by Scottish & Newcastle plc. to the Stout market, being the first new draught Scottish Stout to be launched by this company in recent decades.

The man that isn't jolly after drinking,
Is just a drivelling idiot, to my thinking.
          - Euripides, 480-406 B.C., Cyclops.

The Bear's Head, Brereton

ON THIS DAY IN APRIL...

3rd April 1797
- Thrale and Company are summoned to "answer complaint made against them for making casks on their premises". From the 16th century on only Coopers Company in London have owned the privilege of making all the casks used by the brewers in London.

14th April 1931
- The Royal Commission on the Sale and Supply of Intoxicating Liquors recommends the extension of the State Management Scheme.

THE LAGER PHENOMENON IN BRITAIN, CONT...

Lager brewing was then picked up by another Scottish company, Tennents of Glasgow, who commenced test brews in May 1885, and subsequently constructed a complete lager brewery in 1891. This plan for brewing lager in Glasgow was derided in the local press as "a madman's dream", but Tennents proved them wrong and lager brewing allowed them to survive the First World War and prosper to this day as part of the giant Bass group.

The demand for lager rose rapidly after the Second World War, doubtless due to rise of foreign holidays and the exposure of all things 'continental'. Many British brewers added a lager to their product range albeit with varying degrees of success. Draught lager made an appearance in the mid 1960s further widening the market. Perhaps the true secret of lager's supposed appeal was the real awfulness of many of the competing ale products marketed by British brewers in the 1960s and 70s. Lager reached over 50% of the total market in Britain in the mid 1980s although the tide in the 1990s seems to be receding due to improved ale products and perhaps amid unfavourable publicity attached to lager from the tabloid press. "Lager lout" is a term increasingly attached to some of the less prepossessing elements of society. It is still possible that we might begin to witness a decline in lager as rapid as that of porter at the turn of the present century. Time will tell.

A very early lager label

Drink! for you know not whence you came, nor why;

Drink! for you know not why you go, nor where.

- Omar Khayyam, 1050-1123, Rubaiyat.

The George Inn, Salisbury

ON THIS DAY IN APRIL...

16th April 1936
- A New York brewer begins producing "draught" beer in ½ gallon, 1 gallon and 3∫ gallon cans. The can comes fitted with its own aluminium air pump, faucet, and release valve etc. The dispenser is tapped into a cork bung in the same way as a barrel of beer.

19th April 1879
- Lager beer is first brewed in Britain by William Younger & Co. in Edinburgh.

26th April 1665
- Samuel Pepys records in his diary, "My cold continuing and my stomach sick with the buttered ale that I did drink the last night in bed, which did lie upon me till I did this morning vomit it up".

SAINTLY SPONSORS

THE PATRON SAINT OF INNKEEPERS?

There have been a few nominees to the title of the patron saint of publicans, the discerning drinker can take his choice from the following:

St. Boniface once had his name applied to innkeepers in general. George Farquhar's comic play *The Beaux Strategem* published in 1707 features a humorous scene where the innkeeper introduces himself as:

"Old Will Boniface; pretty well known upon this road. I have now in my cellar ten tun of the best ale in Staffordshire: 'tis smooth as oil, sweet as milk, clear as amber, and strong as brandy. I have fed purely upon ale. I have ate my ale, drank my ale, and I always sleep upon my ale."

The traveller upon asking him how long he has lived entirely upon ale is told:

"Eight and fifty years, upon my credit, sir; but it killed my wife, poor woman. She would not let the ale take its natural course, sir, she was for qualifying it every now and then with a dram, an honest gentleman that came this way from Ireland, made her a present of a dozen bottles of usquebaugh (whisky) - but the poor woman was never well after".

Why innkeepers should popularly have gained the name Boniface is not clear. In Latin it simply means "the well-doer" and was conferred on **St. Winifrith**, an Anglo-Saxon born at Crediton in Devon, in recognition of his life-work of converting the Germanic peoples to Christianity. Although St. Boniface is described by one of his biographers to have been before his conversion "a stout man, addicted to drink" it does seem unlikely to be true. It is more likely that the very sound of the name was the reason for its application to innkeepers. "Bonny face" may have simply reflected the traditional idea of the jolly, good-natured innkeeper.

In older translations of the New Testament **St. Matthew** was described as a "publican" - a word which should have been better translated as tax-gatherer. The term "publican" understandably led to many regarding Matthew as a purveyor of ales. To the extent that one Church of England dignitary used to decorate his church every St. Matthew's Day with hops!

A stronger claimant to the title of patron saint, however, is **St. Theodotus** whose name appears on the calendar on May 18th. St. Theodotus was himself an innkeeper in the city of Ancyra in Galatia where he suffered martyrdom during Roman persecution in the year 303 A.D.

St. Martin also challenges in the role of guardian and protector of the public interest. For the simple reason that the autumn wine-feast of the pagans became confused with the mediæval Feast of St. Martin (November 11th), he became the "patron" of tavern-keepers, wine merchants, and other dispensers of good cheer. No doubt the saintly French bishop would not have approved of appearing alongside the Greek god Bacchus in the hall of the Vintners' Company.

Innkeepers, 1641

There is absolutely no scientific proof of a trustworthy kind, that moderate consumption of sound alcoholic liquor does a healthy body any harm at all; While on the other hand there is the unbroken testimony of all history that alcoholic liquors have been used by the strongest, wisest, handsomest, and in every way best, races of all times.

- **George Saintsbury, 1845-1933,**
Notes on a Cellar-Book.

The Grantley Arms, Wonersh

ON THIS DAY IN APRIL...

26th April 1986
- Brewing ceases at Holyrood Brewery, Edinburgh (William Youngers).

28th April 1841
- Andrew Reid of Griffin Brewery dies. A newspaper reports "It is somewhat remarkable that we have within a few weeks, had to record the death of three of the most celebrated porter brewers of the day. It is equally remarkable that all these gentlemen had reached a patriarchal age".

SAINTLY SPONSORS

MAGIC BROOMSTICKS AND BEER

The English humorist Richard Harris Barham (1788-1845) was a canon of St. Paul's and the writer of the *Ingoldsby Legends*, irreverent comic verse based on mediæval legends. In the *Lay of St. Dunstan* he tells the tale of Peter the Lay-Brother who made a wish and got much more than he bargained for!

Brother Peter obtained the magic broomstick of St. Dunstan and put it to the best use he could think of - to bring him beer to his lonely monastic cell. Off went the broom which at first delivered ale by the flagon, then by the barrel, and finally "started the hoops", deluging the cell with ale faster than the poor monk could drink it. In desperation Peter seizes the broomstick and breaks it in half, only to find that each half continues to deliver beer. The poem is not only still a humorous and cautionary tale but also a list of what was considered some of the best ales of the early 19th century:

> For both now came loaded with Meux's entire;
>
> Combe's, Delafield's, Hanbury's, Truman's, - no stopping -
>
> Goding's, Charrington's, Whitbread's continued to drop in
>
> With Hodson's pale ale, from the Sun Brewhouse, Wapping.

The deluge continues until Peter's brother monks open the door of his cell:

> The Lay-Brothers nearest were up to their necks
>
> In an instant, and swimming in strong double X;
>
> While Peter, who, spite of himself now had drank hard,
>
> After floating awhile, like a toast in a tankard,
>
> To the bottom had sunk,
>
> and was spied by a monk,
>
> Stone-dead, like poor Clarence, half drown'd and half drunk.

A bumper of good liquor
will end a contest quicker
than justice, judge, or vicar.
  - R. B. Sheridan, 1751-1816, The Duenna.

The Angel Inn, Pattison's brewery Woolhampton

ON THIS DAY IN MAY...

29th April 1884
- Death of Michael Thomas Bass, grandson of the founder. His ambition was "to brew the very best beer that could possibly be brewed". It was said that he "was probably more deeply lamented than any other inhabitant of Burton since that place became a town".

1st May 1869
- The Wine and Beer House Act is introduced designed to reduce the number of beer houses which has soared to 53,000 and is rising by about 2,000 a year.

THE BURTON BREW

BURTON AND THE RED TRIANGLE

The town of Burton-on-Trent has long been regarded as the brewing capital of England. Although at one time or another some of the larger cities, such as London, have boasted more breweries in total, nowhere were breweries more concentrated than in Burton. In Saxon and mediæval times the office of Cellarer was one of the most important in English religious houses, and even in the 12th century, Burton-upon-Trent had already gained a reputation for its ale. Before the Reformation the abbot was Lord of the manor, and the abbey and its dependencies were practically the whole town. A local rhyme from the city tells us:

The Abbot of Burton brewed good ale,
on Fridays when they fasted -
But the Abbot of Burton never tasted his own
As long as his neighbour's lasted.

When Mary, Queen of Scots was imprisoned in Tutbury Castle in 1584 she was supplied with beer from "Burton three myles off".

The secret of Burton's reputation came mainly from its water supply passing through gypsum beds in the neighbourhood, which makes it particularly suitable for brewing beer. The town really came into prominence as a centre of brewing in the late 18th century with the introduction of pale ales, for which the hard waters of Burton, were eminently suited.

Among the most famous names associated with brewing in Burton are Allsopp, Eadie, Everard, Marston, Salt, Worthington, and Bass. Demand for Burton ale led to the need for transportation to surrounding areas in an age when road traffic was mainly by pack horse. Two familiar names emerge from this trade. Still known throughout the country the great transport firm of Pickfords was established in 1640 and carried ales for the Burton brewers.

In 1723 a small carrier near Burton used to brew beer in his spare time and sell it while doing his delivery rounds. The demand for his beverage grew to such an extent that in 1777 he sold his carrying business to Pickfords and devoted himself exclusively to brewing beer. By this move William Bass became the founder of one of Burton's most important breweries.

Advertising the "Red Triangle"

So laugh, lads, and quaff, lads,
Twill make you stout and hale;
Through all my days, I'll sing the praise
of Brown October ale.
          - Song from light opera *Robin Hood*,
              1891, by Reginald De Koven.

The Bear's Head, Brereton

ON THIS DAY IN MAY...

7th May 1660
- Samuel Pepys records in his diary, "This morning Captain Cuttace sent me 12 bottles of Margate Ale. Three of them I drank presently with some friends in a coach... After I was in bed Mr. Sheply and W. Howe came. I gave them three bottles of Margate Ale and sat laughing and very merry till one o'clock in the morning".

12th May 1913
- The Right Honourable William McEwan, master brewer, politician and philanthropist, dies. His name had become a byword for quality beer.

15th May 1744
- Porter first brewed outside London. Thomas Elliot of Sheffield advertises in the Leeds Mercury, welcoming orders for his porter "as good as any Brew'd in London".

BURTON AND THE RED TRIANGLE, CONT...

In a history of Staffordshire written in 1686 the author says of the brewers of Burton: "They have a knack of fineing it in three days to a degree that it shall not only be potable, but as clear and palatable as one would desire any drink of the kind to be". Imbibers of earlier times, however, liked their ale much stronger than today's drinkers and reckoned that strong ale made strong men. One Staffordshire innkeeper when asked what made his beer so strong boasted that he "brewed it from women's tongues and men's fists". Then as now alcoholic beverages could be misused and the folly of ascribing machismo to strong or excessive beer drinking is apparently nothing new. Past ages no doubt had their equivalent of today's "lager louts" :

Never tell me of liquors from Spain or from France,
They may get in your heels and inspire you to dance;
But the ale of old Burton, if mellow and right,
Will get in your heads and inspire you to fight.

Burton beers travelled well and kept their clarity in hot climates, and their reputation grew both in the export and domestic markets. "Burton" in fact became a beer much imitated throughout Britain and even further afield in places such as Belgium.

Although some of the other Burton brewers are at least as revered as Bass, additional fame has been imparted to the latter by its instantly recognisable trademark of the Red Triangle.

This is widely regarded as being the world's first registered trade-mark (1876) and its use has been jealously guarded ever since by the parent company (now the giant Bass plc) who have raised lawsuits against anybody sporting a trade-mark which vaguely resembles a red triangle. The origin of the original trade-mark itself is obscure; it has been suggested that the triangle represents a pyramid, as the ancient Egyptians were noted brewers, but this is probably apocryphal. Much more likely is that the triangle was simply one of a whole series of crosses, stars and the like used by brewers since time immemorial, and which are thought to be connected with the ancient aspirations of alchemy.

Beer brewing is not so far removed from alchemy, being the art of producing gold from base materials, in this case liquid gold. Bass's trade-mark has gained added immortality by being depicted in Manet's famous 1882 painting "The Bar at the Folies-Bergeres", in which bottles of Bass can clearly be seen alongside the magnums of champagne on the bar. The fact that Bass Pale Ale could stand alongside such drinks as champagne as an equal is ample testimony to its standing as one of the world's most respected beers.

"The Bar at the Folies-Bergeres", Manet, 1823

The Bermuda Sun

VITAL VICTUALS FOR VICTOR . .

Charity begins at home, and yesterday the Gorch Fock, the German tall ship, was the recipient of 20 cases of German Beck's Beer.

Mr. William Frith of Frith's Liquors, the representatives of Beck's in Bermuda, received a cable telling him to present Captain Hans Engel, the skipper of the Gorch Fock, with the beer free of charge.

The beer was taken to the ship by Mr. Frith who opened the first bottle for Captain Engel.

Beck's are the largest German beer exporters, and have their headquarters in Bremen, one of Germany's principle sea-faring towns.

Beck's, always in demand throughout the world

BECK'S BIER

Beck's Bier must be the most famous German beer in the world.

The tradition of Beck's is a constant one dating back to 1874, when the characteristic clean-tasting classic pilsner beer was first brewed in Bremen under the supervision of Cord. Hinrich Haake. Beck's has always been brewed to Germany's famous Reinheitsgebot - the Pure Beer Law which dates back to 1516, and which only allows the use of water, malts, yeast and hops in the brewing process-and it soon reached a wide and approving audience in its home town, Bremen.

Bremen, the home of Brauerei Beck & Co., is a famous Hanseatic seaport in North Germany. Proud of its independent history (Bremen is still the smallest state in the Federal union that makes up today's Germany), and its trading links with the outside world, it is not surprising that Brauerei Beck & Co. soon looked outside Germany for markets for its beer. Indeed, just two years after it was first brewed, in 1876, Beck's was being exported to the USA and was winning brewing medals in Philadelphia.

The seafaring tradition continues with Beck & Co's sponsorship of the magnificent Schooner, the Alexander von Humboldt

This export phenomenon has continued unabated over the last one hundred years, and Beck's is now sold in over one hundred and forty countries throughout the world, making it far and away Germany's biggest export beer. Central to the development of Beck's has been Brauerei Beck's insistence on always brewing Beck's in Bremen. This consistency is symbolised by the unchanging presentation of the Beck's logo and bottle. The 'Key' trademark, in use since the Brewery's foundation, is derived from the city symbol of Bremen-a trading gateway for the North of Germany. Equally well known is the green bottle, familiar and unchanging throughout the world.

Beck's success story in the UK is of more recent origin. European-style pilsner beers have not traditionally been popular in the UK and, although Beck's has been sold over here since the late 1940's its widespread availability dates from the growth of lager brands in the late 1970's. This interest for classic German style beer has gathered pace over the last fifteen years, and as the British palate has become better able to distinguish quality in this style, Beck's has gone from strength to strength.

The Beck's tradition of unchanging dedication to quality production has led to global fame and a century of success; this same recipe will surely ensure its unrivalled popularity into the 21st century.

It is mighty difficult to get drunk on 2.75 per cent beer.

    - Herbert Hoover, 31st President of U.S.A.
      Statement to the Press, 5 June 1918.

ON THIS DAY IN MAY...

The King's Head, Ombersley

16th May 1955
- Tennents of Glasgow are the first British brewers to adopt 16oz. cans.

18th May
- St. Theodotus day. An innkeeper in the city of Ancyra in Galatia, Theodotus was martyred during the Diocletian Persecution in the year 303 A.D.

20th May 1712
- The reputation of Burton ales is already well established in London and on this day Sir Roger de Coverley visits Vauxhall and enjoys "a glass of Burton ale and a slice of beef".

THE GROWTH OF INNS, TAVERNS AND PUBLIC HOUSES

It could be said that the history of Britain's inns, taverns and public houses reflects the history and progress of the country itself. The birth of the inn came with the first roads, as soon as man had roads to travel the inn was there providing sustenance and a place to stop over. During daylight travelling hours, alehouses sprang up at crossroads to provide travellers with lesser stops for simple refreshments. As the towns grew up along the highways there came the tavern in the town providing for the locals a place to relax after the toil of the day. The coming of industrialisation and mass production then gave us the modern public house.

Time and trends may have changed but over the centuries inns and taverns remain at the centre of social life, reflecting the mood and tastes of the times, accommodating commerce, providing places to meet friends and business associates, places to communicate, to solve problems great and small, at times providing a haven of peace, at times even a place to conspire revolution. No other institution has held such a continuous and intimate contact with the British people through the ages. How many soldiers down through the centuries have echoed the sentiment of the camp-follower in Shakespeare's Henry V?: **"Would I were in an ale-house in London".**

According to a recent survey the attraction of the tavern has not waned. One in four adults visit a public house at least once a week. They are still the most popular places for meeting friends and beer is still top of the drinker's "pops".

Tourists are also fans with nine out of ten Americans preferring British "pubs" to their own hostelries. Among retail outlets the inns and taverns of Britain are still unique in many ways, not the least for providing unpaid tax-collectors! In the 1990s the poor publican is now responsible for collecting over £2.5 billion a year on beer alone and about £630 million on food. The inns and taverns of Britain can truly be said to be a vitally important economic and social part of our way of life.

The word "Inn" is of good Saxon origin, at first simply signifying a room or chamber it later came to be applied generally to a mansion house or stately home. We still have evidence of this meaning in place names such as "Lincoln's Inn" which was once the family home of the Earls of Lincoln, and "Gray's Inn" the town residence of the Lords Gray. Even at the time when it was being generally applied to drinking taverns the word "Inn" was still used to signify a simple boarding-house. The "Inns of Court" in London were originally lodgings for the law students there.

"Tam O'Shanter and Souter Johnny",
Geikie's Etchings

You can only drink 30 or 40 glasses of beer a day, no matter how rich you are.
- Col. Adolphus Busch,
newspaper interview.

The Bell Inn
Waltham St. Lawrence

ON THIS DAY IN MAY...

25th May 1668
- Samuel Pepys records in diary, "Walked to Magdalene College, and there in the butterys, as a stranger, and there drank my belly full of their beer, which pleased me, as the best I ever drank".

26th May 1787
- George III and his Queen visit Samuel Whitbread's Chiswell Street Brewery in London, the first royal visit to a British brewery. It is reported that "Princess Elizabeth, who is fond of mechanics, took several notes in her pocket book while she was in the steam engine room". "You may depend" she tells Miss Whitbread "I shan't set up a rival brewery".

PERSONABLE PUBS AND INVITING INNS

THE INNS OF THE MIDDLE AGES

In the Middle Ages the inns were places of very mixed social classes and offered only the most basic of services. We can see from Chaucer's *Canterbury Tales* how the knight freely socialised in the inn with the miller, the cook, and the ploughman. But it would seem very likely that the travelling pilgrim found little comfort and even less privacy during his stay. Each guest would purchase from the host his requirements, which was generally the traditional diet of the Middle Ages - the "three Bs" - Bread, Beef, and Beer.

It may have been frugal fare but then as now many "hosts" were guilty of exploiting their "guests" and charging extortionate prices. In 1350, therefore, Parliament was forced to intervene to ensure innkeepers charged a reasonable tariff for their wares. The beds, however, could hardly be considered dear at a penny a head in London, and even less in the country inns, while servants were usually charged at half rate.

The traveller, no doubt, still found this over-priced when finding himself faced with the typical inn accommodation - a number of beds placed in a single room and each one invariably over-run with fleas, bugs and other vermin. In only one way did the traveller leave with more than he came with!

THE ALE-HOUSE AND THE ALE-WIFE

In addition to the inns where one could stay the night there was the lesser "alehouse" along the highway where travellers could simply stop for refreshment.

Generally situated at cross-roads the alehouses could be seen from a long way off by means of a common sign. Protruding from above the front door of every alehouse was a long, horizontal pole on which was tied a thick bush. This was called an "Ale Stake" or "Ale Pole" and there are many examples in the literature of the time. Chaucer writing in 1386 tells us:

A garland had he set upon his head

as great as it were an ale-stake.

"Mother Louse", alewife

Or Holinshed in 1587 writes:

Booths and Ale-poles are pitched at St. James his gate.

Some alehouses, in fact, had such a size of ale-pole that in 1375 Parliament passed an Act restricting their size as they were endangering the heads of horsemen riding by.

Then as now, some alehouses had such a bad reputation that topers were reluctant to be seen entering them:

Some, lothe to be espyde

Start in at the back syde

Over the hedge and pale

And all for the good ale.

Outside the religious houses, brewing at the time was largely a domestic industry and generally in the hands of women. The ale-wife was therefore a common figure, but she did not enjoy a particularly flattering reputation, traditionally being depicted as "Mother Louse".

Cider on beer makes good cheer
Beer on cider makes a bad rider.
                     - West Country saying.

The Lygon Arms, Broadway

ON THIS DAY IN MAY/JUN...

1st June 1781
- Dr. Johnson's short participation in the brewing industry comes to an end when Thrale's Brewery, the fourth largest in London, is put up for sale. On assessing its value he pronounces "We are not here to sell a parcel of boilers and vats, but the potentiality of growing rich beyond the dreams of avarice".

4th June 1777
- The Grand Trunk Canal linking the Trent with the Mersey allows Burton brewers to sell beer to the West Coast, Ireland and the America.

CUSTOMER RELATIONS IN THE 16TH CENTURY

The ideal inn or tavern should have a "homely" or "friendly" atmosphere, the innkeeper be a "host" with a customer "the guest". The tradition of our hostelries is one of hospitality, even if it has to be paid for, and even if at times it falls far short of the traditional ideal. Problems with falling short are not new, today managers and staff may be trained in customer relations, in the past they were admonished in other ways. The following recommendations were set out in a 16th century broadsheet and in principle could still provide good advice for any publican:

"Our saviour in the Gospel commends the use of Inns. Yea, Christ Himself by His own presence did sanctify the use of Inns by eating His Passover there.

It must not be a small matter to afford house room, lodging, rest, and food to the comfort of God's children. Though your house (as an Inn) be open for all men to come unto, yet account honest men your best guests.

Because your guests be God's children, let their usage for meat, lodging, diet and sleep be such as becomes worthy personages.

Content yourselves with an honest gain, so using your guests as they may have an appetite to return to you when they are gone from you.

And for your guests, use an Inn as your own house, not to dwell in, but to rest for such a time as ye have just and needful occasion, and then to return in your own families.

Eat and drink for necessity and strength, not for lust. At table let your talk be powdered with the salt of wisdom, as your meat is seasoned. Above all, abhor oaths, cursing and blasphemy."

SUED FOR NOT GOING TO THE PUB

Monday July 26 1993 - Legendary cricketer Ian Botham was sued by Tyneside based Newcastle Breweries for not visiting enough pubs. The former England star had signed a two year deal to promote the breweries' beers by visits to pubs and clubs, but the brewery claimed he had not fulfilled enough engagements. The brewery said:

"When he was there he was absolutely splendid. It is not the quality, but the quantity which is at issue. He always seemed to have too many other commitments".

"I am na fou, I just hae plenty", Geikie's Etchings

FINE TRADITIONAL ALES
AND A GLIMPSE
OF LIVING HISTORY

T & R Theakston has been brewing at Masham on the same site since 1827, when Robert Theakston and his friend, John Wood, set up in partnership together. After five years, John Wood died, but Robert continued the business and proved to be highly successful. During the 1840s, he acquired more inns in the local area, supplying them with his popular ale from the Black Bull brewhouse.

In 1875, business had expanded so much that a new brewhouse and maltings were built and these premises are the same ones which can be seen at Masham today, although inevitaby there have been some changes and alterations since the 19th century. Theakstons became a limited company in 1905 and in 1919 acquired the neighbouring and rival brewery of T. Lightfoot together with its tied properties. For the majority of this century the company continued as a modest local brewery with a relatively small tied estate of some 20 or so local properties, predominantly serving the rural and farming communities of North Yorkshire.

In the early 1970's Theakston acquired the formerly state-run Carlisle brewery and its beers began to reach a much wider market. When Theakston itself was taken over by Matthew Brown in 1983, its ales were commanding considerable national interest, particularly *Old Peculier*, which had become something of a cult brand.

Despite these developments and the subsequent joining with Scottish and Newcastle in 1988, Theakston has managed to maintain its identity and the individuality of its ales. Brewing continues at the Masham Brewery as it has always done and much of the original equipment remains unchanged. Head brewer Hugh Curley oversees both the Masham brewing and quality at Tyne, where Theakston is also produced to meet the increasing demand.

Despite the passage of time and the increasing demand for its products, Theakston has also maintained tradition in the shape of its cooperage, which employs three full time coopers to build and repair the oak casks in which ales from Masham are still distributed. Indeed, the three Theakston craftsmen represent more than 25% of the country's remaining brewery coopers, who now number just 11 - despite there having been thousands employed in the trade as recently as the late fifties.

At Masham, there is a brewery Visitors Centre, where it is possible to watch the coopers at work in their cooperage. The production of a cask is a lengthy and precise business with tools that are unique to the brewery trade, such as trussing adze, croze and Cooper's Devil plus a range of skills to which the youngest cooper at Masham- Peter Coates-is the only apprentice the country.

The casks upon which the coopers' work depends are a valuable commodity- each one being numbered and catalogued. Some barrels still in use are more than eighty years old-such is the enduring quality of the oak from which they are made. The ale cask must be one of the most recyclable forms of packaging still in use anywhere!

The Theakston Cask Ale portfolio has seen some additions in the last decade. The four cask ales which are brewed on a regular basis are *Theakston Best Bitter* (A.B.V. 3.8%), *XB* (A.B.V. 4.5%), *Old Peculier* (A.B.V. 5.6%) and *Traditional Mild* (A.B.V. 3.5%)-which was introduced in 1992 and has rapidly gained a strong following.

The fifth and most recent addition to the portfolio is *Masham Ale* (A.B.V. 6.5%). It was first brewed in a bottle in 1992 and appeared in cask form in August 1993 exclusively for the Yorkshire Dales-selling out its entire brew within two weeks! Because of its popularity cask *Masham Ale* will be brewed at Masham in future as a limited edition guest ale - a wonderful beer for high days and holidays only....so watch out for it.

The strong cask portfolio remains the foundation of Theakstons fame, although the ales have gained nationwide popularity both in cask and in other forms. 165 years on, Robert Theakston would be proud of the way in which his name and his ales have become so famous!

Good ale will make a cat speak.
             - Old English proverb.

The Bull, Dartford

ON THIS DAY IN JUNE...

9th June 1871
- Professor Leone Levi submits a special report to Mr. M. T. Bass showing the number of persons employed in the production and distribution of alcoholic beverages to be around 1,500,000 representing nearly 8% of the estimated adult population.

5th June
- Feast day of St. Boniface, the English saint whose name used to be applied to innkeepers.

THE EVOLUTION OF THE "BRITISH PUB"

"The Pub" is regarded as a peculiarly British phenomenon, much imitated in other countries yet never effectively replicated.

A relatively recent phenomenon, insomuch that the pub did not become recognised as such until the latter part of the last century, its roots go right back to the Middle Ages. The public house as we know it today evolved out of the older inns and alehouses, by way of the taverns of the 17th century. The taverns, as opposed to the inns and alehouses which generally provided for the traveller, were places where local inhabitants could meet and socialise. Tavern life became a feature of the cities and larger towns, and were patronised by people of every social class. Most landlords of such premises brewed their own ale. With the growth of commercial brewing in the 18th century things began to change and the public house began to emerge.

Although initially these merely supplemented the older inns and taverns they quickly gained acceptance and rose to prominence. As their name might suggest, they were in fact simply dwelling houses with some of the rooms opened to the public for the express purpose of consuming drink.

Ale and beer were considered traditional fare at the time, and very much regarded as a foodstuff, mainly because of the poor water supply in many towns. The brewing process boiled out many of the water-borne germs such as cholera and typhoid.

Spirits on the other hand, particularly Dutch Geneva (Gin) which due to its low price had become very popular in the 18th century, were considered the cause of much degradation and misery. The lack of regulations also meant that such establishments were open to abuse; open to all age-groups drunkenness was common even among the very young.

Many of the worst examples were swept away by the Improvement Acts and Licensing Restrictions of the mid 19th century, and the remainder were much more strictly regulated. An Act of 1853 introduced strict hours of closing and imposed a strict division between publicans and licensed grocers. The former were to be debarred from retailing groceries and the latter for selling drink for consumption on the premises.

The Boundary Bar, Leith

Yes my soul sentimentally craves British Beer.

- Thomas Campbell, 1777-1844, Scottish poet.

The Talbot Inn, Chaddesley Corbett

ON THIS DAY IN JUNE...

15th June 1215
- The signing of the Magna Carta. One of the national liberties defined therein is a uniform measure for ale and wine.

28th June 1664
- Samuel Pepys records in his diary, "and thence with my Uncle Wight to the mum house, and there drinking, he do complain of his wife most cruel as the most troublesome woman in the world, and how she will have her will".

THE EVOLUTION OF THE "BRITISH PUB", CONT...

In mid-late Victorian times, in an attempt to civilise the public house and make it respectable, a new type of establishment began to make an appearance, in the larger centres at least.

The trend was mainly set by the brewery owned establishments who, in the expanding markets created by the growing towns, had the resources to create grandiose places of elaborate decor in order to attract the paying customers. The result was the "Palace" pub, a large elegant open-plan establishment, featuring elaborate woodwork, fine etched glass, gilt and mirrors, and with the "bar" a prominent feature.

In stark contrast to the older alehouses, where the publican had generally waited on tables and where it had often been difficult for them to control exactly what was happening in each of the small rooms, the new pubs were high-ceilinged and well lit, often commanded by a grand central island or horseshoe bar. In the urban areas of the North, some street corner public houses of the older type still survive, although they are progressively regulated and more often than not threatened by urban renewal.

The grand "Palace" style of late Victorian and Edwardian times are generally regarded as the apogee of pub design in Britain, and no such readily identifiable style has subsequently overtaken this idea of what a pub should look like. In the 1930s there were a few isolated examples of the prevailing "art-deco" and "moderne" styles, and post World War Two saw the proto-functionalist "New Brutalism", but generally speaking the "Palace" style has prevailed.

The character of the public house has changed significantly, however. The older ones which survived urban redevelopment underwent "modernisation". Out went the women's snugs and the jug-bars, and in came the lounge-bar, television, juke-box and gaming machine. Bar snacks began to be served as a matter of course.

The public house no longer fulfilled quite the same social function in the brave post-war world as it had previously. It is still, however, very much an identifiably British institution, indelibly part of our social fabric with no real foreign counterpart. There is little doubt the British pub will continue to stand the test of time.

The Hawes Inn, South Queensferrry, Scotland

Hops, Reformation, Bays, and Beer
Came into England all in one year.
                    - Old English saying.
                    (Probably refers to 1524).

The Halfway House, Ombersley

ON THIS DAY IN JUNE...

21st June 1529
- Death of John Skelton, poet laureate to Henry VIII. One of his longest poems is to a well known ale-wife of the time, *The Tunning of Eleanour Rumming* who he tells us was:-

"ugly of cheer,

her face all bowsy,

wondrously wrinkled;

Her een bleared,

And she gray-haired.

Her kirtle (skirt) Bristow-red,

With clothes upon her head

That weigh a sow of lead."

29th June 1803
- Whitbread offers the services of their brewery "for the Publick Good in the event of actual invasion".

"REAL ALE" - MYTH OR REALITY?

There is little doubt that one of the major phenomenons of the last three decades in the world of beer has been the rise of the 'Real Ale' movement. From relatively small beginnings in the 1970s it is now widely regarded as the most successful consumers movement of recent times with thousands of active members and many thousands more sympathisers and adherents. Denigrated through much of that time by sceptics and opponents alike as faddist and crankish, it has nevertheless succeeded in making a niche for itself, and now seems to be a permanent feature of the scene.

The movement started in a light-hearted way in response to the corporate strategists of the brewing industry who had decided in the 1950s and 60s that the way forward was by heavily advertised nationally available filtered, pasteurised and carbonated beers, often chilled at the point of sale. These brewery-conditioned 'keg' beers were spawned by the difficult trading conditions of the immediate post-war years, and were very much a product of their time.

During and immediately after the Second World War, the advantages of a stable, inert beer which travelled well, had a long cellar life, and could easily be handled by unskilled bar staff, had obvious attractions. Many service-men overseas had also got used to this type of beer during the war. After the war with much of the dispense equipment in a deplorable state, and full employment levels meaning that it was increasingly difficult to retain skilled staff in the pubs, this type of beer came into its own.

Eleanour Rumming,
ale-wife

No soldier can fight unless he is properly fed on beef and beer.
      - Duke of Marlborough, 1650-1722.

The Mermaid Inn, Rye

ON THIS DAY IN JUN/JUL...

30th June 1883
- Bass & Co. are said to employ 2,250 men and boys and uses 250,000 quarters of malt and 31 cwt. of hops. The amount of business done by the firm in one year is £2,400,000.

7th July 1803
- With the threat of French invasion under Napoleon at its height, Elliot's Stag Brewery in Pimlico drill their draymen morning and evening, rewarding them with strong beer "when they had done their duty".

7th July 1893
- Lord Salisbury objects to a government bill intended to severely limit the number of public houses. He declares he has an "unalterable objection to the fad of making sober people thirsty in order that drunken people may be kept sober".

REAL ALE... REALLY REAL?

REAL ALE - MYTH OR REALITY?, CONT...

There had also been other problems which blighted the brewers at this time. Due to war-time disruption of sea-going commerce much marginal land had been taken under cultivation for barley growing. Unfortunately a good deal of the barley grown on this land was not particularly suitable for brewing, but the brewers had to do the best with what they could get. Raw material, gravity and output restrictions were also still in force not just during the war but well after it had ended. Due to Britain's appalling balance of payments problems, there was an embargo on the importation of foreign malting barley well into the 1950s. Much poor beer was being produced as a result of these problems with low-grade raw materials and defective dispense equipment, and this was coupled with the fact that many breweries themselves had been starved of investment for years due to the difficult trading conditions of the inter-war years and the 1930s depression. The level of beer returns to many breweries was becoming unacceptably high and the attraction of a stable filtered pasteurised beer was obvious to many.

Due to the loss of many export markets during the Second World War, and further retrenchment with de-colonisation, there was substantial over-capacity in the British brewing industry in the 1950s. The domestic market was stagnant too, due to changing tastes and the advent of new innovations such as television which had 'hijacked' many of the potential customers. The scene was set for a process of rationalisation in the industry, consisting of the elimination of many of the smaller units and heavy investment in a few to produce large volumes of keg beers, with the benefits of economies of scale. Beer was still widely regarded as a foodstuff, and this trend towards a convenience beer was little different from that of the trend towards convenience foods.

Cobblers and tinkers are the best ale drinkers.
- Old English proverb.

The Mermaid, Rye

ON THIS DAY IN JULY...

11th July 1797
- The famous actor and comedian Charles Macklin dies at the age of 97. His final performance was as Shylock at the age of 91. He put his health and longevity down to a daily pint of hot stout.

13th July 1631
- Dorchester Corporation receives complaints about the drays of the city's brewers disturbing traffic.

"REAL ALE" - MYTH OR REALITY?, CONT...

Although not necessarily consumer led, the move towards keg beers was a trend broadly welcomed by the consumer, who had been having to put up with some rather erratic beers for some years, and who welcomed a product that was at least stable and consistent. Red Barrel, Long Life, Double Diamond, Whitbread Tankard and Tartan Bitter were some of the most successful stories of the 1960s.

By the 1970s something of a reaction was beginning to set in as realisation dawned that the new beers were weaker, gassier and more expensive than the traditional cask and draught ales. As these cask ales, often catering for strictly local tastes, were withdrawn or simply disappeared more people began to search out the dwindling number of traditional 'real' ales, brewed without filtrations and pasteurisation and without the introduction of carbon-dioxide. In most cases these older beers compared more than favourably with their keg counterparts, but the breweries were by now understandably reluctant to recognise this belated demand for the types of beers which no longer fitted in with their corporate strategies, and which they were busy trying to phase out.

Undoubtedly the most successful of these movements has been CAMRA, the Campaign for Real Ale, launched in 1971. The 'Real Ale' part of the title is something of a misnomer as all ale is 'real', at least when it is brewed, although given the lack of any strict and binding definitions in Britain of what beer actually is, this is perhaps debatable. CAMRA has fought for drinkers to have a real choice between keg beers, lagers, or unpressurised traditional cask beer. Although in percentage terms, cask ale still forms only a small share of the total market, CAMRA's relative success can be judged from the fact that all the major breweries now produce at least one or more cask ale, and a host of small micro-breweries have been set up to produce cask beer.

A number of the larger brewing companies have also been forced to rethink their keg-only products, and products such as Watney's Red (nee Red Barrel) have now disappeared entirely from the market.

So will cask-conditioned real ales make a complete comeback and oust keg beers and lagers completely? Very doubtful! Keg beers and lagers are here to stay, they have obvious advantages for those premises which don't have proper cellar facilities or have low turnovers. CAMRA's greatest success has been in persuading the brewers to offer the consumer a choice. It is also true that some drinkers now like the tang associated with carbonated keg beers, and wouldn't thank you for Crudgington's 6X Gold Medal Bitter, or Honker & McNasty's 120/- Ale. The actual brewing process, and the chemical changes that take place therein are practically unchanged since time immemorial, although enhanced scientific understanding of the process coupled with technical innovations have resulted in the beers being produced much more rapidly. But beer remains much the same, and all beers are real, some are just more real than others.

CAMPAIGN FOR REAL ALE

ABBEY BREWERY, EDINBURGH c. 1890.

WILLIAM YOUNGER & CO. LTD

William Younger established his first brewery in Leith, Edinburgh's port, in 1749, and within a few decades moved to larger premises in Edinburgh itself, where over the succeeding few centuries the company he founded grew to become one of Britain's largest and most famous brewing concerns. William Younger & Co. Ltd. exported their beer widely, and were known the world over for their ales, beers and stouts. In 1931 Younger's merged with another Edinburgh brewing comapny, McEwan's, to form Scottish Brewers Ltd., and today are part of Scottish & Newcastle plc.

One of the beers for which Wm. Younger & Co. became justifiably famous was *I.P.A., India Pale Ale.* This light sparkling beer was originally produced especially for the overseas and colonial markets, and in particular the large expatriate and military markets of the Indian sub-continent, hence the name, but it also became in time, very popular on the domestic market, where it is still available today. *Youngers I.P.A.* is a 4.5% A.B.V. beer, and is particularly favoured in Yorkshire, the English Midlands, and the South of England.

Another very famous Younger's beer, and one which is market leader for its type in Cumbria and Yorkshire, is *Younger's Scotch Bitter*. This very pleasing middle gravity ale of 3.7% A.B.V. is now being made available in both cask-conditioned and new mixed-gas form, making it suitable for all types of outlets.

Younger's No 3 is a unique, dark coloured, strong, traditional ale brewed by William Younger's since the 1800's when it was identified as No.3L, signifying that it was exported to London.

It compliments this range of beer and ensures that the name of William Younger & Co. Ltd., under the famous 'Father William' trademark (that lively old gentleman who "gets Younger every day"), will continue to be known the length and breadth of Britain as the company approaches the 250th anniversary of its foundation in 1749.

Beer drinking don't do half the harm of lovemaking.

      - Eden Philpotts, *The Farmer's Wife.*

ON THIS DAY IN JULY...

The King's Head, Aylesbury

14th July 1936
- Hospital of St. Cross, Winchester celebrates its 800th anniversary. A ration of free beer and bread has been served on demand to every genuine wayfarer for 800 years, a custom begun by Henri de Blois, the brother of King Stephen, in 1136.

20th July 1577
- A census of the exact number of ale-houses, taverns and inns in England and Wales comes to a total of 19,759. The estimated population is around 3,700,000 which means that there is one licence for every 187 persons. The highest number by far is in Yorkshire which accounts for nearly 20% of the country's total.

THE ALE - CONNER'S ART

In Mediæval times the scientific understanding of the brewing process was somewhat limited, and attempts both to measure the strength of ales and raise excise duties on those strengths tended to be rather rule of thumb affairs. In England, Henry III's attempts to raise revenue through the Assize of Ale of 1267 met with opposition from the brewers, who simply reduced the strengths of their ales in order to avoid having to pay more duty. In those days, given the absence of hops which were still to be introduced to these islands, English ales tended to be stronger and sweeter than they are now and had a much higher level of residual sugar.

One way of testing the strength of the ales was to measure the sugar content. This was the job of the "Ale-Conner", who, centuries before the invention of the saccharimeter, devised a much cruder method of assessment. This involved a small measure of the ale which was to be tested and a pair of leather breeches. The measure of ale was poured on to a wooden bench and the Ale-Conner sat in it in his leather breeches. Having wriggled himself around for a while, he was then required to sit still for a predetermined period of time. When he moved to get up, if his leather breeches stuck to the bench, the ale was then adjudged to be of an acceptable strength! It is doubtful if this would be employed today, if only because the leather breeches would prove rather expensive, but there are now more scientific methods available for assessing the strength of your beer.

Ale-Conners

Religions change, beer and wine remain.
- Harvey Allen, 1889-1949,
Anthony Adverse.

The Star Inn, Alfriston

ON THIS DAY IN JULY...

23rd July 1830
- The Beer House Act more or less permits anyone the right to retail beer for an annual cost of two guineas, "for the better supplying of the public".

28th July 1914
- The First World War begins. Its repercussions are to have a profound effect on brewing both in Britain and Ireland.

BOTTLED ALE

THE ORIGINS OF BOTTLED BEER

Alexander Newell, Dean of St. Pauls and master of Westminster School, in the reign of Mary Tudor, seems to have been as keen on his beer as he was on his angling.

The Bishop of London, Edward Bonner, however, was no respecter of Alexander Newell. Bonner led the Counter Reformation in England and was responsible for burning a number of Protestants. One day while Newell was fishing at his favourite spot on the banks of the Thames he received the warning that the Bloody Bishop was after him. With no time to return to his house Newell made for the coast and fled the country.

Several years later, after the death of Mary Tudor and the imprisonment of Bonner, Newell made his return to England and his old haunts. He remembered that on that fateful fishing trip before he fled the country, like any good angler, he had taken provision with him for the day. Returning to the bank he searched and found the bottle of beer which he had safely stashed away many years before. On sitting down to celebrate his find, the historian Thomas Fuller tells us, "He found it no bottle, but a gun - such was the sound at opening thereof". Fuller writing in the 17th century reckoned that "this is the origin of bottled ale in England".

DRIVEN TO DRINK

July 31st 1993 - Drivers abandoned their cars in droves in Hanover, Germany when a beer tanker truck overturned. As 23,000 gallons of beer gushed out, a queue of people filled bottles, cups, jars, flasks and any container they could find, with the amber liquid. The "free round" lasted for hours until rain eventually spoiled the beer.

DRAUGHT or BOTTLED BEER?

VOTE for DRAUGHT

VOTE for BOTTLED

Which is the best long drink in the world?

St. George he was for England,
and before he killed the dragon.
He drank a pint of English ale
Out of an English flagon.
                    - G.K. Chesterton, 1874-1936,
                              The Englishman.

The George, Huntingdon

ON THIS DAY IN JULY...

30th July 1422
- The Masters of the Brewers' Company in London are imprisoned and fined for attempting to keep the price of beer artificially high. The complainant against the Company is the former Lord Mayor of London, Dick Whittington.

31st July 1923
- The Intoxicating Liquor Act sets the age limit for alcohol at 18 years of age.

EDINBURGH - BRITAIN'S CAPITAL OF BREWING?

Few British towns have as long and illustrious a brewing pedigree as does Edinburgh. Although Burton has laid claim to being the brewing capital of Britain, when compared to Scotland's capital its claim looks a little hollow. Brewing started in Edinburgh with the monks of Holyrood Abbey as early as the 12th century, and by the 16th century commercial brewing was sufficiently well established for a powerful Society of Brewers to be formed to regulate the trade. This body, the forerunner of many later similar bodies elsewhere, were responsible for the organisation of the piping of brewing water and the supply of good quality malting barley. By the 18th century, with the opening of new markets following the Act of Union, some of the most famous names in Scottish brewing had become established. Names such as Drybroughs, Campbells and Youngers would be familiar for two centuries and more. At its peak in the latter part of the 19th century, Edinburgh could boast some forty breweries. Upwards of a dozen were situated in the Canongate alone, that ancient thoroughfare in the very heart of the Old Town which stretches from the High Street to Holyrood Abbey.

The secret of Edinburgh's success as a centre of brewing came from the fine brewing water available from an underground trough which ringed the city and came to be known as "The Charmed Circle". This supply of hard water was very suitable for brewing, particularly for the Pale Ales which came much into vogue in the 19th century both for the domestic and export markets. These beers travelled well and kept their clarity in hot climates, and thus became very popular for the overseas colonial and military markets in particular. Edinburgh Ales became famous the world over, and were synonymous with quality. It may be difficult to imagine now but at its peak Edinburgh Ale was probably more famous throughout the world than Scotch whisky. It was this fame which maintained the industry largely intact through the difficult days of the inter-war years.

Edinburgh Castle from the Grassmarket

THE BEER DRINKER'S COMPANION

Good ale, the true and proper drink of Englishmen. He is not deserving of the name of Englishman who speaketh against ale, that is good ale.

- George Borrow, *Lavengro*, 1851.

The Spread Eagle, Midhurst

ON THIS DAY IN JUL/AUG...

4th August 1788
- Deacon William Brodie, the original Dr. Jekyll, and his accomplice meet in Edinburgh to drink Black Cork and plan the robbery of the Excise Office for Scotland.

4th August 1812
- The first food-canning factory is established in London.

EDINBURGH - BRITAIN'S CAPITAL OF BREWING?, CONT...

Although a process of rationalisation and amalgamation had been taking place gradually in the city since at least the turn of the century, as late as 1960 there were still nearly thirty breweries in Edinburgh, thereafter, however, a rapid contraction took place. The reasons for this were many and varied, but crucial was the Edinburgh brewers' long dependence on the export markets, which declined sharply after World War Two with the hastening end of colonialism. The result was that many breweries were working well under capacity. This and a stagnant domestic market meant many companies were ripe for takeover. Attempts at achieving a measure of rationalisation amongst themselves failed, and this allowed the Edinburgh brewery companies to be picked off one-by-one by predators mostly from south of England or overseas. In the decade between 1960 and 1970 the number of breweries was more than halved to seven. By 1990 that was down to three, and by 1993 only two breweries and one very small pub-brewery remained.

This decline is not only sad in employment terms for the city, but also in the fact that Edinburgh, which could once claim to be Britain's most prominent brewing centre, now has so little to show for it. While Burton has the splendid Bass Museum and Heritage Centre, as well as the Heritage Brewery, a working Victorian brewery museum, Edinburgh's attempts to establish a similar Archive and Heritage Centre has met with only lukewarm support.

In 1992 the historical records and artifacts of Edinburgh's brewing history were removed to Glasgow, a city with a negligible brewing tradition in comparison, a sad postscript to Edinburgh's undoubted stature in world, not just British brewing.

The Holyrood brewery, 1890

Drink today, and drown all sorrow,
You shall perhaps not do it tomorrow:
Best, while you have it, use your breath;
There is no drinking after death.
                    - John Fletcher, 1579-1625, The
                                    Bloody Brother.

Corner of Gallery, George Inn,
Dorchester

ON THIS DAY IN AUGUST...

10th August 1418
- During the Hundred Years War while King Henry V lays siege to Rouen, he sends a message back to London asking for urgent supplies to be sent to his troops. The Lord Mayor duly obliges and despatches 30 butts of wine, 1,000 pipes of ale and 2,500 cups.

14th August 1834
- The Beer House Amendment Act distinguishes between "on" and "off" licenses.

BEFUDDLED BREWING

THE STATE AND BREWING IN BRITAIN

In Britain the brewing industry has always been overwhelmingly in private hands, and while the state has sought to regulate the industry from time to time - the recent Monopolies & Mergers Commission Report is one example - it has for the most part refrained from any direct involvement. It is not so well known, however, that in three small enclaves in Britain the state's involvement was total, from production to retail. This experiment, which its proponents hoped would be extended to cover the whole of Britain, operated modestly and successfully for more than half of the present century.

The story really starts with the First World War. Under the 1915 Defence of the Realm Act (DORA) restorations were placed on brewers in terms of raw materials, gravities and output. One result of this was the much derided "Munitions Ale", a weak beer of low gravity designed not to hamper the war effort. Curbs on licensing hours were also introduced, but in late 1915 there came the "Shell Scandal" on the Western Front, when the failure of a British advance was blamed on a shortage of shells. The wily Lloyd George, Minister of Munitions, sought to blame this on the evils of drink, which was of course in line with the Liberal Party's pre-war adherence to the Temperance cause.

Three strategic areas of Britain were recognised as being vital to the war effort; the Carlisle - Gretna area where there were numerous munitions factories; the Enfield area of Middlesex where there was a famous armaments factory (Lee-Enfield rifles etc.); and the Invergordon - Cromarty area in North - East Scotland where there was an important naval base and dockyard. Accordingly, in January 1916, it was decreed that these areas be taken under direct state control by way of compulsory purchase. All licensed premises, breweries, wine and spirit stores and the like in these areas were acquired, and a process of rationalisation begun. Almost half the pubs in the areas were closed and others improved to sell a range of food and non-alcoholic beverages. Billiard rooms and reading rooms were introduced, and in some instances even cinemas and bowling greens. A strict "no-treating" role was initiated, making the buying of rounds of drinks expressly forbidden, single drinks only being sold for individual consumption.

beer is best

FOUNTAIN BREWERY, EDINBURGH c.1885.

WM. MCEWAN & CO. LTD

William McEwan, the son of an Alloa shipowner, established his famous Fountain Brewery at Fountainbridge on the west side of Edinburgh in 1856. The name of the brewery and the area was derived from the spring waters in the vicinity, and within a few decades McEwans's had established an enviable reputation as one of the foremost brewing concerns in Scotland. Today more beers appear under the McEwan name than any other brand-name.

Much of William McEwan's early success was built on the reputation of his Export Ale. With the help of his family's shipowning connections, William McEwan began exporting ales and beers from the early 1860's, supplying the large military and colonial markets of the Empire. McEwan's beers travelled well and kept their clarity in hot climates, and were much in demand in the overseas markets, using the traditional Scottish shilling numerology of 60/-, 70/-, 80/- and the like, this being the late 19th century invoice price per barrel.

Whilst William McEwan himself retired from active participation in the company in the late 1880s to concentrate on a career in politics, later becoming M.P. for the Edinburgh Central Division, the company went from strength to strength, eventually merging with fellow Edinburgh brewers Wm. Younger & Co. Ltd. in 1931 to form Scottish Brewers Ltd. Today as part of Scottish & Newcastle plc., a range of products are still produced under the McEwan's name at the Fountain Brewery in Edinburgh, bearing the traditional Hand-and-Globe, Crossed-Flags, and Cavalier logos which have long been the company's trademarks.

McEwan's Export, 70/- & 80/- Ales are perennial beers which have stood the test of time. *McEwan's Export*, as exported to the colonies, has long been the flagship brand as a 4.5% A.B.V. brewery-conditioned and packaged beer, and *McEwan's 80/- Ale* (also 4.5% A.B.V.) which is Scotland's biggest selling cask beer, and has nearly a century and a half of tradition to reinforce its appeal. *McEwan's 70/-* Ale is another beer with a long pedigree, and has recently been launched as a mixed-gas product as well as the exisiting cask product. This medium gravity traditional Scottish Ale at 3.7% A.B.V. will appeal to those who favour a session beer, and is available to publicans as an alternative to the higher gravity *McEwan's 80/-*.

McEwan's has long been regarded as one of Scotland's, indeed Britain's, foremost breweries and is synonymous with quality in beer throughout the world. Today the McEwan's name continues to embody all the characteristics of quality and tradition which has made it famous since its inception in 1850.

Give me a bumper, fill it up:
See how it sparkles in the cup;
O how shall I regale!
Can any taste this drink divine,
And then compare rum, brandy, wine,
Or aught with nappy Ale?
  - John Gay, *A Ballad on Ale,* 1720.

ON THIS DAY IN AUGUST...

The Mitre, Oxford

15th August 1920
- The *Brewers' Journal* inaugurates a campaign for the collective publicity of beer - "Beer is Best".

17th August 1921
- The Licensing Act introduces new opening hours. They are fixed at a maximum of nine hours in one day in London and eight hours elsewhere. The times are left to the decision of the local Justices of the Peace.

BEFUDDLED BREWING

THE STATE AND BREWING IN BRITAIN, CONT...

The largest of these districts, the Solway area, encompassed the towns of Carlisle, Gretna, Annan, Longtown, Silloth and Maryport, and covered an area of nearly 500 square miles with five breweries and nearly 400 public houses initially. By the end of the war only one brewery remained in operation, and in terms of curbing drunkenness and enhancing the war effort the whole exercise was adjudged a modest success.

After the end of the First World War this experiment was allowed to continue in these areas, whereas throughout the country as a whole the war-time curbs were gradually lifted. Nevertheless it was hoped in some quarters that eventually this system would be extended nationwide. A 1931 Royal Commission on the State and Supply of Intoxicating Liquors recommended just this course of action, but the private brewing industry lobby was too powerful and nothing further was done. The State Management Districts, however, were allowed to continue serenely into the post Second World War era, now under the control of the Home Secretary (the Scottish Secretary in Scotland). As late as the 1950s the then Home Secretary in the MacMillan government, Sir David Maxwell-Fyfe, pressed for State Management to be extended to the New Towns then under construction on both sides of the border, but nothing was done, and, when the Conservatives returned to power under Edward Heath in 1971, these areas were eventually returned to the private sector.

Thus ended in Britain the State's lone incursion into control of the brewing industry. The experiment had lasted fifty-five years and its demise was greatly mourned in the areas affected, not least because drink was retailed at substantially below the national average. In the country as a whole, however, many persons were unaware of the existence of these areas and their passing went largely unnoticed. An inauspicious end to a promising experiment.

I would give all my fame for a pot of ale and safety.

    - Shakespeare, *Henry V*, Act v, sc 4.

The Anchor Inn, Liphook

ON THIS DAY IN AUGUST...

19th August 1773
- Dr. Johnson observes that drinking less than our ancestors is owing to the change from ale to wine. "I remember," said he" "when all the *decent* people in Lichfield got drunk every night, and were not the worse thought of. Ale was cheap, so you pressed strongly. When a man must bring a bottle of wine, he is not in such haste". (From Boswell's *Journal of a Tour to the Hebrides with Samuel Johnson*).

24th August 1782
- Brewer Robert Barclay writes to the firm of Boulton and Watt asking for a visit to his brewery and advice on installing one of their "Fire Mills" (steam engine).

BREWING AND TRANSPORT

At the time during the 18th century when commercial brewing was becoming established in Britain, the transport infrastructure was very poor. Most breweries therefore used, as far as possible, local raw materials (barley, malt, coal etc.) and supplied strictly local markets. There was a limit to how many baskets of malt or how many barrels of beer could be sent by cart or pack-horse. Sea transport was certainly much in use, however, both for domestic and export purposes.

From at least the 1780s, and possibly earlier, beer was sent overseas to destinations such as the Americas, the Baltic ports, and the Colonies, a hogshead or two initially going as part of a general cargo. Coastal traffic around the shores of Britain was very prevalent too. The London brewers, for example, despatched whole cargoes of puncheons of Porter to slake the thirsts of colliers and the like in northern sea-towns such as Newcastle. Many small breweries were situated by the sea, where they could be easily supplied with raw materials and in turn despatch the finished product.

The brewers of Burton, an inland town with fine brewing water, were largely restricted to local markets until the completion of the Trent and Mersey Canal in 1777 gave them access to the sea and allowed them to supply Liverpool, Cardiff, Bristol, London and the Americas. Later canal construction gave them links to the Humber, allowing them to supply east coast ports and on to Russia. Similarly, the Forth and Clyde Canal in Scotland, completed in 1790, allowed the products of the Edinburgh and Alloa brewers to reach the west coast without the hazardous trip around the north of Scotland. For internal transport the canals held sway until the coming of the railways midway through the following century. Although their role then declined they were still being used in some areas until well after the Second World War, only then did motor transport sound the final death knell for the canals.

In the winter of 1822 the brewers of Edinburgh, which already included such famous names as Campbells, Drybroughs, and Youngers, were in serious trouble. A spell of bad weather had meant that the roads from the Lothian coalfield, virtually on the city's doorstep, were impassable. High seas had also closed the port of Leith to the coal-ships, and the Forth and Clyde canal was frozen solid. The populace of Edinburgh, cold and hungry, were on the point of starvation, and even worse, little beer was being brewed. Coal was vital for heating and boiling purposes in the breweries and beer was very much regarded as a foodstuff in those days.

A one-horse power Will Younger's Dray Cart from about 1860

A double glass o' the inwariable.
   - Charles Dickens, Pickwick Papers, *1836.*

The White Horse, Eaton Soccon

ON THIS DAY IN AUG/SEP...

1st September 1659
- Edinburgh's council imposes further duty on the price of ale sold within the city bounds, thus raising it to the unheard of price of one penny a pint! John Nicoll is not, according to his diary, the only one displeased at this action. When the time comes for the duty to come into effect he writes, "at the same instant God frae the heavens declared his anger by sending thunder, and unheard tempests, and storms, and inundations of water... to the town's great charges and expenses".

9th September 1871
- On a visit to Whitbread's brewery in London, the famous French chemist Louis Pasteur is amazed at its size and writes, "It is impossible to get any idea of its immensity. It produces 305,000 barrels of beer a year, and employs 250 workmen and 100 horses".

TORTUOUS TRANSPORT

BREWING AND TRANSPORT, CONT...

The result was the Edinburgh-Dalkeith Railway, a link between the Lothian coalfields and the city. Commissioned by Act of Parliament in 1826 it was opened in 1831. Over the next few decades the railways spread until a network covered most of Britain. The transport of beer became an important part of many railway companies' traffic, with specially constructed slatted cask wagons, yeast vans, and in later years, beer tanker wagons. Some large brewery concerns, such as Bass in Burton and Guinness in Dublin had their own internal railway systems with their own locomotives and rolling stock and miles of track.

Most, however, simply had railway sidings and perhaps a locomotive with a few wagons. The railways had a somewhat double-edged effect, although they greatly extended the markets of the larger brewers, in turn the coming of the railway exposed some of the smaller country brewers to the full force of competition from their larger urban counterparts who enjoyed cost advantages in the form of economies of scale. This resulted in the elimination of many smaller breweries.

One railway anecdote which deserves recourse is the story of a train called "The Newcastle Beer". This was a regular service which conveyed the products of the Edinburgh breweries to the thirsty drinkers of the north-east of England. To avoid added congestion on the east coast main line, this train was routed over the difficult Border Counties line, which ran over the wild fells of Northumberland. On one occasion on those bleak northern fells in the very depth of winter, there was a derailment and several wagons overturned with many casks broken open. So cold was the temperature on this particular night that despite the alcoholic content, the spilled beer actually froze solid. News of this act of providence quickly reached the ears of the local populace, who quickly began arriving on the scene in substantial numbers, armed with jugs, cans and pannikins, which they filled up with frozen beer chipped away from the spillage. In a part of the world where such events take on perhaps added significance, this occurrence was talked about for many years afterwards, becoming part of the local folklore.

Early motor transport at Holyrood brewery

The One and Only
NEWCASTLE
SERVE COOL
550ml
BROWN ALE
ALCOHOL 4.7% VOL

NEWCASTLE BROWN ALE

At the 39th Annual General Meeting of The Newcastle Breweries Ltd., in 1924, the Chairman, Barras Ramsey Reed spoke of the increasing demand for bottled beers. Already, in strict secrecy, trial brews were taking place of a new bottled beer that was formulated to meet north-eastern tastes, but which would in time spread far outwith its original confines, to become a beer of almost legendary proportions.

This was *Newcastle Brown Ale*, The 'Broon' of legend, in its distinctive clear flint glass shouldered bottle with the famous Blue Star trademark. The brainchild of Head Brewer Lt. Col. James H. Porter, and Newcastle Breweries Chief Chemist Archie Jones, the beer was three years in the preparation, to make sure it was exactly what the public wanted, and it was April 1927 before it went on sale.

Newcastle Brown Ale, a medium-strong, reddish brown ale with a quite unique flavour and aroma, was an immediate success, and at the 1928 Brewer's Exhibition in London won the prestigious Challenge Cup for the best bottled beer. By 1930 the Board of Directors of the Newcastle Breweries were able to report that bottled beer sales had increased by 30% over the previous year's figures, with a substantial proportion of this increase accounted for by Newcastle Brown Ale. Shortly thereafter James H. Porter became a Director himself, and eventually Chairman of the Newcastle Breweries Ltd.

Newcastle Brown Ale continued its success story over succeeding decades, and the merger in 1960 of Scottish Brewers Ltd. with The Newcastle Breweries Ltd. to form Scottish & Newcastle Breweries Ltd., enabled the product to reach a much wider market

Newcastle Brown Ale had always been a bottled beer, but by the 1960's was also made available in a can for the off-sales trade. At a time when bottled beers sales were declining dramatically in the 1970's and 80's, *Newcastle Brown* significantly bucked the trend, becoming something of a cult product. The unique nature of the product-no other was quite like it-meant that it was eclectic in appeal, and crossed all boundaries, appealing to ale drinkers and bottled lager drinkers alike. By the 1980's it had become a big seller in the South of England, and achieved true national brand status, and in addition had a substantial export presence.

With the growth of premium bottled beers in the later 1980's and into the 90's, *Newcastle Brown Ale* was well placed to take advantage of this trend, and sales have soared, with more than ninety million pint bottles being produced at the Tyne Brewery every year.

A significant proportion of the total output, some 16% at present and rising, is now exported to over forty countries. The USA is a particularly big market for *Newcastle Brown Ale*, and new markets are being developed in the former Eastern Block countries. On the domestic market, a new 330ml. (12fl.oz.) bottle has been produced for the off-trade, while the distinctive 550ml. clear glass pint bottle will remain unique for discerning beer drinkers. Commemorative labels have always been a feature of *Newcastle Brown Ale* and have recently been produced for the Tall Ships Race (1986 & 1993), the Gateshead Garden Festival, and to celebrate Newcastle United's triumphant ascent to the football Premier League.

Newcastle Brown Ale is only brewed at the Tyne Brewery, and as exported worldwide is identical in every way with the domestic product which has now been continuously brewed for the last sixty years. There is little doubt that *Newcastle Brown Ale* is a major success story in the history of British brewing, and looks set to continue so for many years to come.

God made yeast, as well as dough, and loves fermentation just as dearly as he loves vegetation.

- Ralph Waldo Emerson, 1803-82.

The King's Head, Malmesbury

ON THIS DAY IN SEPTEMBER...

10th September 1551
- Six commoners of the City of London are appointed "hop-searchers" by an Act of the Lord Mayor. Their job is to seize and burn any hops found to be "not holsome for man's bodie".

11th September 1731
- *Applebie's Journal* tells of an old gentleman "near ninety" who puts his good health down to the good English breakfasts he had in his youth, "good hams, cold sirloin and good beer".

BREWING AND TRANSPORT, CONT...

Some brewery companies had supplemented horse-drays with early motor and steam lorries for local deliveries, from at least the First World War. In the years following World War Two, the motor lorry becoming faster, more reliable and able to carry greater capacities, gradually began to take over from rail transport. Fowlers of Prestonpans, brewers of the famed 'Wee Heavy', for example, used to send its motor draymen delivering right round the North of Scotland in the 1950s on Monday to Friday lodging turns. Horse-drays survived, however, for local deliveries in many places until well into the 1960s.

Sea-traffic also lasted a long time, with brewers such as Jas. Deuchar of Montrose, Calder of Alloa, and Wm. Younger of Edinburgh all shipping beer by sea down the east coast to destinations such as Newcastle, Sunderland, Hull, and London until at least the Second World War. In February 1945, for example, the S.S. Egholm was sunk with a full cargo of Youngers beer for military export whilst on passage from Leith to London. The cargo consisted of 61 hogsheads (54 gallons), 215 barrels (36 gallons), 361 kilderkins (18 gallons), 264 firkins (9 gallons) and 52 pins (4 gallons). In March that year an almost equivalent cargo was lost when the S.S. Chrightoun was mined and sank. Nowadays, however, sea-borne transport is restricted to incoming barley shipments.

Today, sea transport, the canals and the railways seem to all have had their day as far as beer transport is concerned. Most beer is now transported by bulk road tanker, with motor-drays for local deliveries, although some enterprising brewery companies, such as Youngs of Wandsworth and Vaux of Sunderland retain splendid teams of horse-drawn drays for this purpose. It is doubtful, however, if the trends towards tradition in the brewing industry will result in the wholesale re-introduction of the horse.

Clipper ship "Swiftsure", 1326 Tons.

*Your best barley wine, the good liquor that
our honest forefathers did use to drink of.*
      - Izaak Walton, *The Complete Angler.*

The Lygon Arms,

ON THIS DAY IN SEPTEMBER...

12th September 1945
- The Second World War ends. The influence of American tastes are about to change British beer.

15th September 1895
- The Pattison saga begins when Pattison, Elder & Co. start up their Duddingston New Brewery, near Edinburgh.

24th September 1493
The Edinburgh Society awards Bartholomew Bell, brewer, a Silver Medal in recognition of the excellence of his Black Cork beer.

WILLIAM McEWAN - MASTER BREWER

William McEwan was born in the famous Scottish brewing town of Alloa in 1827. His association with the trade must have started early, his father was a local shipowner and his consignments must have included many a hogshead of Alloa ale. His sister had also married into the famous Alloa brewing family, Youngers. On leaving school he worked briefly in Alloa, Glasgow and Huddersfield before settling in Edinburgh.

In 1851 he started to learn the trade at Jeffrey's Heriot Brewery in the Grassmarket. After five years, and with the financial help of his Younger in-laws, William McEwan left to establish his own brewery on the west side of Edinburgh.

Situated at Fountainbridge the chosen site was conveniently located between the Union Canal, which linked Edinburgh to Glasgow, and the Caledonian Railway. The Fountain Brewery of Wm. McEwan & Co. was opened in 1856. Its good transport links gave it a marked advantage over many of its competitors, and within a few years a sizable trade had been built up with the expanding industrial areas of the west of Scotland and Tyneside. In the early 1860s the expansion went even further and McEwan's began exporting beers to overseas markets. Hence "Export" and "Pale India" ales were born, with India, Australia, New Zealand and the West Indies becoming the main markets. McEwan's ales travelled well on long sea voyages and also kept their condition in hot climates.

By the 1880s the Fountain Brewery had expanded considerably to become one of the leading brewing concerns in the country, becoming a Limited Company in 1889 with a capital of £1 million.

Although he still kept his position as Company Chairman, McEwan had retired from active participation in the business after 1886 to concentrate on his political career.

The success of his efforts had left him a very wealthy man. He died, aged 86 years old, at his London town house in 1913, leaving a personal fortune of over £1.5 million.

William McEwan was the very epitome of the enterprising and vigorous Victorian entrepreneur. Although the family line has died out, his name still lives both in the brewery he founded and in the fine ale tradition which bears his name.

William McEwan

We lived for days on nothing but food and water.
                              - W. C. Fields.

The Swan, Tetsworth

ON THIS DAY IN SEPTEMBER...

24th September 1946
- H.M.S. Menestheus is officially decommissioned.

24th September 1493
- Beer brewers achieve the distinction of being officially recognised as a guild.

28th September 1660
- Samuel Pepys records in his diary, "I did send for a cup of tea (a China drink) of which I had never drank before". Tea at the time costs around £3 a pound, a sum more than a year's wages for many people.

VIGOROUS VICTORIANS

THE FOUNTAIN BREWERY, EDINBURGH

William McEwan chose his new brewery site wisely when building started at Fountainbridge in 1856. The four wells sunk on the site lay within Edinburgh's "charmed circle", a geological fault containing the purest of fresh water covered by a thin layer of sandstone. The Caledonian Railway ran past the new buildings and a rail siding was laid directly into the brewery making it easy for coal and barley to be shipped in and the finished products shunted out. The Union Canal also lay about a hundred yards from the main gates. The site was ideal for not only producing quality ale but also for market expansion.

Unusually amongst Scottish brewers, there were initially no maltings at the Fountain Brewery, malt being purchased from outside suppliers. All expansion was concentrated on brewing capacity and the Fountainbridge beers were exported to every part of the British Empire, and eventually to South America. By 1880 the Fountain Brewery covered 12 acres and employed hundreds of workers.

The two world wars proved to be difficult times for the brewery and, as the colonial countries gained their independence, the home market became the main target. In the 1950s the famous cans of "McEwan's Export" became a brand leader.

Long famous for its imposing clock tower, the older Fountain Brewery was replaced by a much more modern plant on the south side of Fountainbridge in 1973. With its high speed canning line the new brewery cost Scottish & Newcastle £13 million. The clock, so well known to Fountainbridge residents, was retained, as well as the name the "Fountain Brewery" and the McEwan trade name. The brewery is still a tribute to the foresight and vision of the founder William McEwan who established his world famous ales nearly a century and a half ago.

The Fountain brewery

The only advantage of having lived through the Age of Prohibition is that any liquor tastes good.

- Don Marquis, 1878-1937,
American journalist.

Porch room at The George, Salisbury

ON THIS DAY IN SEP/OCT...

29th September 1736
- The Gin Act come into force. Gin is so cheap prior to the act that signs read "Get drunk for a penny, dead drunk for twopence". The government imposes a tax of 20s. on a gallon of gin and sets the retailer's licence at £50. Gin drinkers throughout the country are enraged and the guards are doubled at Kensington Palace, Whitehall and other areas in London in fear of riots.

1st October 1788
- Deacon William Brodie, the original Dr. Jekyll, is executed in Edinburgh's High Street, the first man to be hanged on a gibbet he himself had designed.

THE McEWAN HALL - GRADUATIONS, CONCERTS AND BEER

In 1884, at the Tercentenary of the foundation of the University of Edinburgh, an appeal was launched for funds to enable the completione of an extension to the University. The prominent local brewer and philanthropist William McEwan contributed £1,500 and was consequently invited to join the Appeal Committee.

There was in addition to the University extensions a great need for a suitable graduation hall, and in 1886 William McEwan suggested to the University authorities that if they were to acquire land adjacent to the new university buildings, he would pay for the erection on the site of the graduation hall. The scheme was approved and work began in 1888, the University having also decided that the completed building should be called the McEwan Hall in recognition of Mr. McEwan's generosity.

By the time of its completion in 1897 the total cost of erection and furbishment was £115,000. The sum was met in full by William McEwan, who stipulated that the hall should in addition be used for civic ceremonies by the City of Edinburgh where appropriate. The University agreed and an organ was installed so that it could also be used for concerts. This too was at McEwan's expense, as well as a further grant of £6,500 per annum for the upkeep and maintenance of the hall.

Semi-circular in plan and seating 2,200, the hall was designed in early Italian Renaissance style by R. Rowand Anderson, and it has remained little changed since it was completed in 1897. Two former graduates adorn the sides of the stage: to the left is a profile of Sir Walter Scott with the admonition "Watch weel"; to the right is Thomas Carlyle, with the words "Work and despair not".

The McEwan Hall still provides a scene of grandeur for the University of Edinburgh graduation ceremonies.

McEwan Hall (Courtesy of McEwan's Alehouse, Edinburgh)

As I brew, so I must drink.
             - Old English proverb.

The King's Head, Chigwell

ON THIS DAY IN OCTOBER...

4th October 1661
- Samuel Pepys records in his diary, "Then Captain Ferrers and I to the theatre... we staid not to see it out, but went out and drank a bottle or two of China Ale".

8th October 1698
- John Coachman, servant to brewer Timothy Burrell, receives his wages. Burrell's journal records, "Payd John Coachman, in full of his half-year wages, £2. 6s. 6d., to be spent in ale".

WILLIAM McEWAN - POLITICIAN AND PHILANTHROPIST

By the 1880s William McEwan's brewing interests had made him a very wealthy man. In the General Election of 1886 he stood as a Liberal, and easily won the seat for Edinburgh Central Division against the Unionist candidate. In Parliament he became a staunch supporter of Prime Minister William Gladstone. Although he came out strongly in favour of Irish Home Rule he also predicted its downfall, because "he knew the people".

He won the seat again in 1892, this time against a Labour & Temperance candidate as well as a Unionist. He seems to have been a highly respected constituency M.P., for when he won the seat for the third time in the 1895 General Election he was totally unopposed. By this time, it is said, he had even won the support of the local Temperance lobby. A remarkable feat indeed for a man who had made his fortune from brewing!

During this time McEwan had also acquired a deserved reputation as a philanthropist and public benefactor, and a supporter of worthy causes. In 1897 he made a gift to the City and University of Edinburgh of the splendid McEwan Hall. In recognition of his generosity, he was given the Freedom of the City of Edinburgh and awarded an Honorary Degree by the University of Edinburgh. Among his many other gifts were a Rembrandt painting to the National Gallery, and £16,000 he left in his will to the Royal Infirmary of Edinburgh. He was described at the time as a "good, kindly, popular man who is . . . exceedingly rich, though he has devoted much money to charity".

Due to ill health he declined to fight his Parliamentary seat in 1900 and after fourteen years retired from Parliament. He declined a peerage but was made a Privy Councillor in 1907.

(Courtesy of McEwan's Alehouse, Edinburgh)

Ale sellers should not be tale tellers.
                    - Old Scots proverb.

Yard of the George Inn, Dorchester

ON THIS DAY IN OCTOBER...

8th October 1919
- Prohibition laws ban alcohol in the United States of America.

10th October 1808
- Samuel Allsopp, brewer in Burton-on-Trent declares his emphasis is for quality not quantity, "I am not an advocate for doing a vast deal of business... I had rather do less and do it well".

THE YOUNGER DYNASTIES

One of the most famous names in British brewing is that of Youngers, a name famous in "The Beerage", and one which has spawned several Cabinet Ministers. Yet as late as the early 1960s there was no less than three separate brewery companies bearing the Youngers name, and this was the source of much confusion amongst the public and the cause of many an argument in pub and club.

Arguments abound as to which of the three companies was the oldest, but we must go back to the mid 18th century to seek an answer. It is claimed that William Younger opened his first brewery at Leith near Edinburgh in 1749. This would have made him barely sixteen years old at the time. It is beyond doubt, however, that William Younger was a brewer in Leith for many years prior to his death in 1770. Over the succeeding two centuries Wm. Younger & Co. grew to become one of the largest brewing firms in Britain, enjoying a large part of both the domestic and export markets. The direct Youngers line of descent continued in brewing with this family until the 1980s, by which time the company was part of Scottish & Newcastle Breweries plc., then one of Britain's "Big Six" brewers. Beers are, however, still marketed today under the Wm. Youngers name, although the Youngers breweries in Edinburgh (Abbey and Holyrood) are now both closed. It was in 1927 that Wm. Younger & Co. Ltd., commissioned the famous artist Arthur Leete to produce "Father William" a cheery old chap with a long white beard, who by drinking the products of the company "Got Younger Every Day".

From the same period in the mid 18th century an entirely unrelated family also entered brewing when George Younger established his brewery in the famous brewing town of Alloa. This event has variously been ascribed to the years 1740 or 1762, but what is certain is that Geo. Younger & Sons grew to become one of the largest brewery companies in Scotland, and continued under family control until its takeover in 1960. This brewing company was also well known the world over, due to its large export military trade, and a keen sense of loss was felt in Alloa when the Candleriggs Brewery closed in 1963.

William Younger, the founder

Look into the pewter pot
To see the world as the world's not.
                    - A. E. Houseman,
                 A Shropshire Lad, 1896.

The George Inn, Dorchester

ON THIS DAY IN OCTOBER...

17th October 1814
- The Meux Brewery disaster takes place. A 20,000 gallon vat bursts, sweeping away tenements and buildings and killing 8 people "by drowning, injury, poisoning by fumes and by drunkeness".

18th October 1864
- Richard Taylor, Ale-taster for Rossendale resigns his post stating that, "I, Richard Taylor, by appointment for the last five years Ale-taster for that part of Her majesty's dominions called Rossendale, do hereby tender my resignation to hold that office after this day, as I am wishful, while young and active, and as my talents are required in another sphere of usefulness, to devote them to that purpose".

VIGOROUS VICTORIANS

THE YOUNGER DYNASTIES, CONT...

Youngers of Alloa have been chiefly known in recent years for having begat the erstwhile Cabinet Minister and Defence Secretary, George (Lord) Younger, a direct descendent of the original George Younger, the 18th century Alloa brewer. Paradoxically the Alloa Youngers were related by marriage to William Younger's deadly Edinburgh rivals, William McEwan & Co. Ltd. Despite the rivalry, William Younger later joined with McEwans to form Scottish Brewers Ltd.

The third Younger brewery was the St. Ann's Brewery, Edinburgh, of Robert Younger. Although situated only a stones throw from the Abbey Brewery of William Younger, he was no relation whatsoever, but was indeed a scion of the Alloa Youngers. This company was taken over by Scottish Brewers Ltd. (i.e. Wm. Younger & McEwans) in late 1960, thereby joining the "enemy camp".

Confusing isn't it? Poor George Younger, when he entered Parliament as Scottish Secretary in the 1980s, was forever being heckled in the House by Opposition M.P.s with cries of "a pint of Tartan Special George!". It was fairly pointless pointing out that they had the wrong "Younger", one from a different family altogether, who just also happened to be involved in brewing and called Younger.

Tavern signs

*While beer brings gladness, don't forget
That water only makes you wet.*
  - Harry Leon Wilson, *The Spenders.*

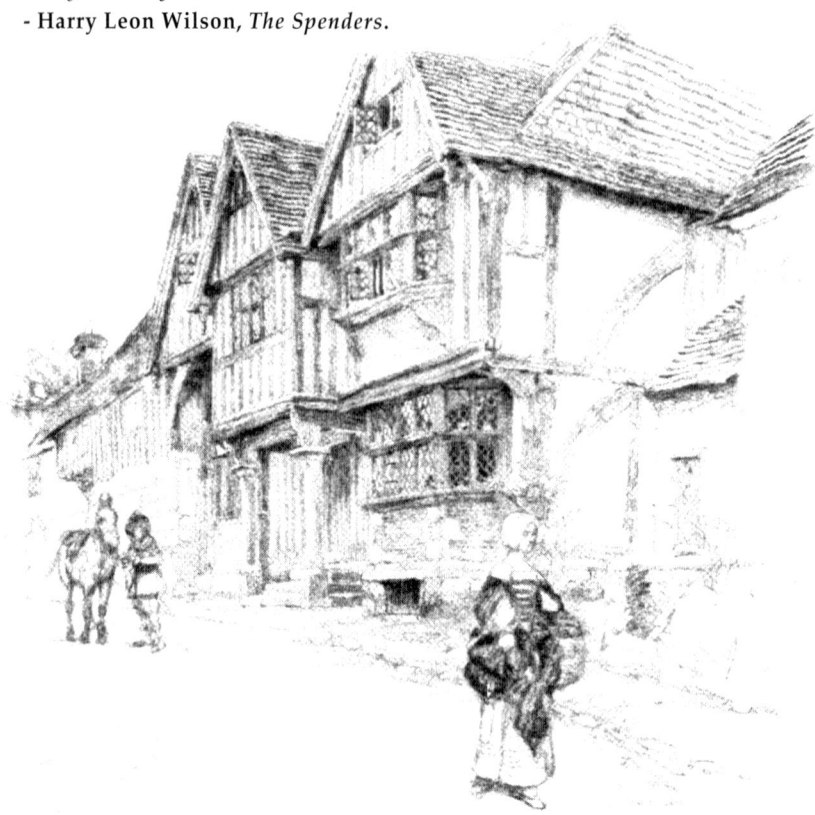

ON THIS DAY IN OCTOBER...   *Chiddingstone*

31st October 1715
- The first of the "Mug-house Riots". Many of those supporters of the loyalist Hanoverian cause who frequent London ale-houses form themselves into Mug-house Clubs and, in an age of violent political struggles, see themselves as champions of law and order, albeit in a very illegal and disorderly manner. Confrontation between the Hanoverian and Jacobite clubs leads to a series of violent street riots between the two factions.

20th October 1936
- Judge (Sir Edward) Parry advises, "From the earliest times governors who did not understand the psychology of the Englishman, and who failed to supply him with good beer, in tankards of reasonable size, at a fair price, have found themselves in trouble. I remember that an outstanding illustration of this fact occurred in 1917. Grave discontent had arisen in Manchester and their industrial area in the Northwest, and I was sent on a mission there to inquire into the causes. I found that the beer shortage was at the root of the unrest".

HIGHLAND HEATHER

HEATHER ALE - THE SECRET OF THE PICTS

In Scotland, legend has it that in ancient times the Picts were noted brewers of a beverage called Heather Ale. The secret of this brew had thought to have been lost in the mists of time. That is until an enterprising Glasgow home-brew supplier, Bruce Williams, began his years of painstaking research to finally rediscover the secret of "Leann Fraoch", Gaelic for Heather Ale. The legendary brew went back into production in a small brewery in the Highlands and was put on sale in selected pubs in Glasgow and Edinburgh.

Although thought of primarily as a distilling nation, Scotland has a long history of brewing which stretches back well beyond that of whisky distilling. Using the raw materials available to them, darnel (corn-weed) and bere (wild coarse barley), the ancient indigenous population made a crude kind of ale from fermented grain with the addition of such things as heather, spruce, rowan, broom and myrica.

The fame of Heather Ale was such that the legend has it that in the 4th century, the High King of Ireland, Niall of the Nine Hostages, led a primitive expedition into south-west Scotland for the express purpose of discovering the secret of Heather Ale. The attempt failed and the King returned to Ireland minus the precious secret. Heather Ale survived for centuries before gradually being replaced by the spread of hop-based beers from continental Europe.

Mug-house riots

Back and side go bare, go bare;
Both foot and hand go cold;
But, belly, God send thee good ale enough,
Whether it be new or old.
   - John Still, Gammer Gurton's Needle, 1575.

The Chequers Inn, Tonbridge

ON THIS DAY IN OCT/NOV...

23rd October 1775
- The fame of Burton ale is international. Brewers B. Wilson & Co. of Burton-on-Trent write to a company in St. Petersburg in Russia, "Many merchants from St. Petersburg are supplied with Burton ale from our house, and there are many whose orders are transmitted through Hull and London".

3rd November 1601
- Sir George Moore in a Parliamentary debate regarding the proposed restrictions on the number of inns and taverns declares, "An Inn is a man's inheritance, and they set at great rates, and therefore, not to be taken away from any particular man".

HEATHER ALE - THE SECRET OF THE PICTS, CONT...

Nevertheless, the legend of Heather Ale remained strong, and in the late 19th century Robert Louis Stevenson even sang its praises -

> From the Bonny Bells of Heather
> They Brewed a Drink Langsyne
> Was Sweeter Far than Honey
> Was Stronger Far than Wine

Although it is claimed that ales of this type were brewed in some of the more outlying areas of Scotland such as the North West Highlands, Galloway and Orkney until the turn of the present century, there is little firm evidence to support the claim. Various attempts have been made to recreate the legendary brew, notably by the famous Scottish writer the late Marian McNeill, but with little success. The breakthrough occurred only in the late 1980s when an old woman from the Western Isles supplied Bruce Williams with an ancient and hitherto jealously guarded recipe which had been handed down through generations. Several years of experimentation followed before Bruce felt confident enough to put his Heather Ale into production.

In July 1993 the first batch of "Leann Fraoch" was produced at Dick Saunders' West Highland Brewery at Taynuilt in Argyllshire. The recipe is, of course, still a well guarded secret but it is known to contain bell and ling heather, myrica (myrtle) and honey as well as the more traditional ingredients of barley, malt, water and yeast. If the strength of the legend is anything to go by, Heather Ale could once again become Scotland's brew.

Ancient Celt Drinking Cup

When treading London's well-known ground
If e'er I feel my spirits tire,
I haul my sail, look up around,
In search of Whitbread's best entire.
              - Anonymous, *A Pot of Porter, Ho!*

The Catherine Wheel, Southwark

ON THIS DAY IN NOVEMBER...

9th November 1666
- Samuel Pepys records in his diary, "We to cards, till two in the morning, and drinking lamb's wool".

9th November 1841
- A new structure is erected at Salt and Co.'s brewery and to celebrate the event a supper is given to the men. In the midst of it the good news comes that the Queen has given birth to a son. In honour of Her Majesty's first born, a huge vat is christened "The Prince of Wales". Twenty-five years later, when on a visit to the brewery, his Royal Highness has the satisfaction of drinking a glass of stout drawn from his namesake.

DAVY JONES BREWERY

BREWING WITH SEA WATER!

Towards the end of the Second World War, the supply lines to the Far East were dangerously stretched. For the forces engaged in the fighting against the Japanese, certain supplies, such as beer were a rare luxury. In order to maintain morale, and at the instigation of Winston Churchill himself, in late 1944 the Board of the Admiralty decided to convert two mine-laying vessels into Amenity Ships, to include cinemas, dance-halls, shops, bars, and on-board breweries.

These two vessels, HMS Menestheus and HMS Agamemnon, were both large ex-Blue Funnel liners which had been converted to mine-laying on the outbreak of war. In early 1945 both vessels were despatched to Vancouver in Canada to be refitted as floating breweries, with brewing plant supplied from the U.K. by the well-known company Adlams of Bristol.

Distilled sea-water was to be used for brewing purposes, and malt extract and hop concentrate would be shipped from the U.K. to bases in the Far East where the vessels would call. A 55 barrel capacity brewing copper was to be installed in the forward hold of the ships and heated by steam coils from the ships' own boilers. Six glass-lined fermenting vessels were also installed, and the capacity was an estimated 250 barrels per week. Only one beer was to be produced - a chilled and carbonated 1037 gravity Mild Ale. Besides being sold in the ships' bars, this was also to be made available in 5 gallon stainless steel kegs.

As some of the brewing kit went missing in transit to Canada, in the final event some of the equipment earmarked for HMS Agamemnon was purloined for its sister ship. On the 31st December 1945 the first trial brew was put through on HMS Menestheus and judged sufficiently successful for brewing to continue. Despite the fact that the war in the Far East had now ended, the Menestheus prepared for her maiden voyage. In January 1946 she left the west coast of Canada to sail across the Pacific bound for Japan, China and Hong Kong, by then all in the hands of British and Allied troops. Yokohama, Kure, Shanghai and Hong Kong were visited in that order, with the latter proving a conspicuous success. Brewing took place at sea in between the ports of call, and was supplied in kegs to other vessel's canteens on arrival at its destination, as well as being sold to the armed forces personnel. The beer was retailed at 9d per pint, or 30/- per 5 gallon keg, and proved surprising popular.

From "Kay's Portraits"

How easy can the barley-bree
Cement the quarrel!
It's aye the cheapest lawyer's fee
To taste the barrel.
      - Robert Burns, 1759-1796, *Scotch Drink.*

The King's Arms, Ombersley

ON THIS DAY IN NOVEMBER...

11th November 1918
- The First World War ends. With British brewers having undergone serious wartime restrictions on their production, the Irish Stout brewers have gained a strong position in the market.

20th November 1944
- Prime Minister Winston Churchill instructs the Secretary for State for War to, "Press on. Make sure that the beer - four pints a week - goes to troops under the fire of the enemy before any of the parties in the rear gets a drop".

DAVY JONES BREWERY

BREWING WITH SEA WATER, CONT...

Japan's unconditional surrender, following the dropping of the atomic bombs on Hiroshima and Nagasaki, made the whole concept rather redundant and the sister ship HMS Agamemnon was never completed. Menestheus sailed for home in June 1946, and after stops at Trincomalee, Aden, Malta, and Gibraltar, it docked at Portsmouth in August 1946. The vessel was then declared officially surplus to requirements, and was decommissioned on the Tyne in September of that year. Thus ended a brief but fascinating episode in British brewing history, although it is doubtful whether any of the beer was ever available in Britain! Nevertheless, in the difficult year of 1946 it did much to slake the thirsts of British and Allied servicemen stationed overseas.

The subsequent history of the vessel is unknown, but some of the brewing equipment was later purchased by the redoubtable John Calder, (who could never resist second-hand brewing equipment at knock-down prices in whatever form it came) and doubtless later appeared in some guise or another in Allsopps, Arrols, Showells, Strettons, or one of the other breweries over which he cast his spell.

Here with my beer I sit,
While golden moments flit:
Alas! they pass unheeded by:
And as they fly,
I, being dry, sit, idly sipping here
My beer.
                    - George Arnold, *Beer.*

The King's Head (Maypole), Chigwell

ON THIS DAY IN NOVEMBER...

27th November 1914
- Defence of the Realm Act imposes stringent restrictions on British brewers but exempts those in Ireland.

30th November 1830
- William Lewis of Llandismaw dies "in the act of drinking a cup of Welsh ale, containing about a wine quart, called a 'tumbler maur'. He made it a rule, every morning of his life to read so many chapters of the Bible and in the evening to drink eight gallons of ale. It is calculated that in his lifetime he must have drunk a sufficient quantity to float a seventy-four gun ship. His size was astonishing, and he weighed forty stone. Although he dies in his parlour, it is found necessary to construct a machine in the form of a crane, to lift his body in a carriage, and afterwards to have the machine to let him down into the grave".

ALE QUENCHERS

Ale may be the best thirst quencher but there at least two instances on record of ale being used as a fire quencher. One January in the seventeenth century occurred a devastating blaze which burnt down the greater portion of the Temple in the neighbourhood of Pump Court. "The night was bitterly cold" writes Mr. Jefferson in *Law and Lawyers*, "and the Templars, aroused from their beds to preserve life and property, could not get an adequate supply of water from the Thames, which the unusual severity of the season had frozen. In this difficulty they actually brought barrels of ale from the Temple batteries and fed the engines with the malt liquor."

In the year 1613 the Globe Theatre was burnt down in consequence of the wadding from a canon fired off during the performance of Henry VIII setting fire to the thatched roof. Fortunately there were no casualties but Sir Henry Watton giving an account of the occurrence wrote "one man had his breeches set on fire that perhaps had broiled him if he had not by the benefit of a provident wit put it out with bottle ale."

For drink, there was beer which was very strong when not mingled with water, but was agreeable to those who were used to it. They drank this with a reed, out of the vessel that held the beer, upon which they saw the barley swim.

- Xenophon, c.435 - c.354 B.C., Greek historian.

The Golden Cross, Oxford

ON THIS DAY IN NOV/DEC...

1st December 1937
- An inn in Prague begins selling its wares "by the hour". By paying the equivalent of fourpence British money the customer is allowed to drink as much as he wants for an hour. The price of any hour after that dropped to the equivalent of twopence an hour. The innkeeper reports his premises are now crowded day and night.

3rd December 1897
- The opening of the magnificent McEwan Hall in Edinburgh, as a graduation hall for Edinburgh University and as a concert hall for the city. The total cost of £115,000 is met by the brewer and politician William McEwan.

CANS, CASKS AND KEGS

THE HISTORY OF BEER IN A CAN

The recent resurgence of canned beer, brought about by such innovations as the "Draught flow" system and the "Widget in the Can", has once again focused attention on this type of container, which became something of a post-war phenomenon.

Food canning had been known since the early 19th century, but it was over a century later that beer was first tried in cans. First experiments took place in the USA in the mid 1930s, in the wake of the lifting of Prohibition. The Kreuger Brewing Company of Newark, New Jersey, started selling canned beer to the public in January 1935. This experiment proved so successful that within the next few years numerous other American brewers followed suit. The can had the distinct advantage of being unbreakable, as well as being lighter and more compact. The fact that it was impervious to light was also an important consideration. The American public, with its liking for filtered and carbonated beers, embraced the idea with enthusiasm.

The British public, on the other hand were a rather different proposition. The British drinker was less used to this type of beer and still wed to the traditional unfiltered and unpasteurised draught ales. News of the American success with canned beer, however, quickly spread across the Atlantic, and within a short time British brewers were also experimenting. British brewers, with their large export trade to the far outposts of the Empire, found the canning of beer especially attractive as freight charges were determined by weight and space. Whilst the first American cans had been "flat-tops", the British cans were "cone-tops", which allowed them (in theory) to be fitted and capped on existing bottling lines.

The first British brewer to produce beer in cans was the small Felinfoel Brewing Company of Llanelli in South Wales, in January 1936. Felinfoel had strong links with the South Wales steel industry, and there was an existing can-manufacturing plant nearby. Brewers such as McEwans, Barclays and Tennents, all of whom had substantial export trades, quickly followed suit. There was, however, a mixed response on the domestic market. Drinkers complained that the cans imparted a metallic taste to the beer, and due to their similarity to the cans in which metal-polish was sold, they were derisively dubbed "Brasso Cans".

With the onset of the Second World War, can production stopped for the domestic market, although canned beer continued to be supplied to those Allied troops serving in distant theatres of war. When the war was over cans made a slow reappearance on the domestic scene before really coming into prominence in the mid 1950s. The take-home trade in beer increased enormously in the 1950s and cans - non-deposit, non-returnable and easily disposable had advantages over the bottle. The British public was also becoming more used to pasteurised and carbonated beers, with the appearance of keg-beers, which were in effect simply larger scaled canned beers. Nevertheless, a significant proportion of the British drinkers were still suspicious of canned beer complaining they tasted "tinny", and that they were difficult to open. By now the British brewers had moved away from cone-top to flat-top cans, but special openers had to be supplied which punched holes in the top of the cans.

Here sleeps in peace a Hampshire grenadier,
Who caught his death by drinking cold small beer;
Soldiers, take heed from his untimely fall,
And when you're hot, drink strong, or not at all.

   - Epitaph on Thomas Thetcher, Grenadier in
   the North Regiment of Hants. Militia. Died
   1764, May 12th.

The New Inn, Gloucester, in 1825

ON THIS DAY IN DECEMBER...

4th December 1935
- Ending of prohibition in the United States of America.

6th December 1717
- Sir Richard Steele writes to his wife saying, "I went to bed last night after taking only a little broth; and all the day before a little tea and bread and butter, with two glasses of mum and a piece of bread at the House of Commons. Temperance and your company, as agreeable as you can take it, will make life tolerable if not easy, even with the gout".

CANS, CASKS AND KEGS

THE HISTORY OF BEER IN A CAN, CONT...

Various innovations took place throughout the 1960s and 70s. The original cans had been 10 fl.oz. for the domestic market and 12 fl.oz. for export. Somewhat surprisingly the industry eventually standardised on the 16 oz. can. This was a rather strange measure in Britain, being little more than ∫ an imperial pint, but the measure took off. Even big 4 pint "Party Cans" made an appearance, whilst improved seamless and subsequently one-piece cans also appeared. The final triumph was the invention of the ring-pull opener which replaced the old can piercers which had to be supplied with purchases. The can became the complete convenience container - unbreakable, easily opened and virtually glass shaped.

Britain's export markets in beer declined sharply after World War Two with the retreat from colonialism, and while beer in cans was still much in demand for ships' stores (Britain still having a large merchant navy at the time), the brewers increasingly turned their attention to the domestic markets.

Several brands of canned beer were heavily advertised, "Long Life", "Double Diamond" and "McEwans" Export, being but a few. These sparkling keg ales, also available in draught form, were the types of beers which went well in cans, but the real success story was LAGER! As a filtered, pasteurised and carbonated beer, not too heavy, the perfect drink on a hot day or to complement a meal - lager was the ideal canned beer. The can and lager were almost mutually supportive: the can enabled lager to reach a much wider market, and lager itself popularised the can. The Glasgow firm of Tennents, for example, now part of the giant Bass group, achieved great success with their canned lagers.

Stouts and Pale Ales were also canned but by the 1980s, with the growth of cheap supermarket "own brands" on the one hand and fashionable "designer" bottled beers and cask-conditioned real ales on the other, canned beer began to experience somewhat of a decline. Many premium beers and cask ales were not suitable for canning, and as lager drinking began to recede, enthusiasm for canned beer began to wane. Some brewers even closed their canning lines and bottles began to make a comeback. In an attempt to stem the ebb away from canned beer, new innovations were introduced aimed at making canned beer more akin to cask ales, the latter being a growth sector in a broadly declining market.

This move seems to have achieved some measure of success, if only in stemming the tide away from canned beer. Nevertheless, cans are here to stay, they still sell massively, but many sales are now restricted to the lower end of the market - both price and gravity wise - where competition is keenest and profit margins low. The trend away from beer in cans probably only mirrors that of other foodstuffs. As the 21st century approaches, the success story of canned beer, if not its long term future, looks a little tarnished. Perhaps Brasso could polish up its image.

Give my people plenty of beer, good beer, and cheap beer, and you will have no revolution among them.
                                    - Queen Victoria.

King John's Palace, Colnbrook

ON THIS DAY IN DECEMBER...

4th December 1935
- First British canned beer is sold by Felinfoel Brewery Co. Ltd., Llanelli, South Wales.

10th December 1773
- Irish brewers complain that the "London brewers have now nearly engrossed the whole trade in Dublin and send their own factors to sell beer to the retailers.

25th December
- An ancient custom at Piddle Hinton in Dorsetshire is for the Rector to give away on Christmas Day a pound of bread, a pint of ale and a mince pie to every poor person in the parish.

FLEMISH FLAVOURS

BELGIUM - A COUNTRY OF BEER

If there is one country in Europe which matches or perhaps even surpasses Britain for the sheer variety of its beer types, then it has to be Belgium. There Red Beers, Cherry Beers, White Beers, Lambic Beers, Wheat Beers and Trappist Beers are brewed which have no real British equivalents, whilst Pale Ales, Pilsner Beers, Stouts and even Scotch Ales are widely available, either imported from Britain or brewed on licence or to the British recipe in Belgium itself. Most Belgian beers are, however, considerably stronger than their British counterparts, the median gravity usually being in the 5.0% - 7.0% ABV range. This was probably a legacy of the period immediately after the First World War, when spirit sales were banned from the ubiquitous Belgian Cafe, and strong beers became much in demand as an alternative.

Traditionally the brewing links between Britain and Belgium are strong, linked by the fact that the two countries are the main producers of top-fermented beers. It should not be forgotten that it was Flemish immigrants from what is now Belgium who crossed the Channel in the 16th century and introduced the aromatic, stringent and preservative qualities of the plant Humulus Lupulus (otherwise known as the Hop) to the British brewers, enabling them to convert many ales into a drink called "beer" from the Flemish "bier". Although British beers have been exported to Belgium for many decades, the Belgian beers that were until recently available here were bottom-fermented lagers and pilsners. Now, however, with increasing levels of discernment among British beer drinkers, some of the unique Belgian top-fermented ales are finding their way into this country.

Belgian beers have a whole range of colours, styles, tastes and densities. In Britain, although the brewing tradition is commonly held to have derived from monastic orders who arrived here from continental Europe, this monastic tradition of brewing has long since died out. Not so in Belgium, where what are known as Trappist Beers are still extensively brewed in religious establishments, abbeys and monasteries, by the Cistercians and other orders to a traditional formulae dating back over centuries. Westmalle, Chinay and Orval are some of the most famous names in the tradition, but there are some fifteen or so monasteries currently licensed to produce Trappist beers, although in some cases licensing agreements are made with small local breweries. Trappist beers, although they vary in taste and colour, are strong and top-fermented and have no real British equivalents.

Neither do perhaps the most unusual and idiosyncratic of Belgian beers, the spontaneously-fermenting "wild" Lambic Beers of the Payoffenland to the south of Brussels. With these beers no yeast is pitched in the brewing process, fermentation instead relying on air-borne wild yeasts. This ancient brewing method, which utilises wheat as a raw material, also produces a beer called Gueuze, a mixture of young fresher Lambics with older well matured Lambic beers. Younger Lambics are cloudy and acidic in nature, whilst the older Lambic beers are clearer and sweeter.

Guinness is Good For You.
> *- Ascribed to Dorothy L. Sayers of
> S.H. Benson Agency, 1929.*

The George Inn, Salisbury 1834

ON THIS DAY IN DECEMBER...

27th December 1822
- Louis Pasteur, French chemist and microbiologist, is born at Dole in France. In 1864, while investigating the problems of fermentation in beer and wine, Pasteur, on examining two vats containing good and bad beer discovers that the "souring" of the beer is due to organisms being introduced from the atmosphere. He then goes on to prove the existence of air-borne germs and becomes the most renowned chemist of his day.

FLEMISH FLAVOURS

BELGIUM - A COUNTRY OF BEER, CONT...

Also cloudy in character are White Beers, most closely associated with East Flanders. Brewed from wheat, these are generally of lower gravity than many Belgian ales, and are often brewed specially as summer ales. Wheat Beers can be similar but are usually stronger. There is a strong tradition of wheat brewing in continental Europe, but it has not extended to Britain, where wheat beers are virtually unknown. Belgian white and wheat beers are top-fermented.

The ruby coloured Red Beers of West Flanders also have no real British equivalent. They are produced by mixing a regular darkish top-fermented brew which uses dark malted barley with a similar brew which has been allowed to mature for 18 months or so. The end result is a sharp and slightly sour beer with a very individualistic and acerbic taste. The Brown Beers of the Oudenaarde and Ghent areas are, on the other hand, rather more like some British beers, although invariably much stronger. These can vary considerably in colour from dark amber to nearly black, and these top-fermented beers usually have a fairly dry aftertaste.

Again, Cherry and other fruit beers are little produced in Britain, although they have been attempted from time to time. Whole cherries (or raspberries or strawberries) are added to an existing wheat-based Lambic brew, and allowed to marinate for several months. Eventually the fruit dissolves, and the resultant admixture can be drawn off. This is then further matured to a point where the fruitiness imparted perfectly balances the acidity of the Lambic original.

Although most Belgian beers are relatively strong, what the Belgians call Strong Ale is often very strong indeed, at times in the region of 10% or more ABV. Pale Ale, in Britain a relatively low gravity drink, also is much stronger in Belgium, even in the variants imported from Britain which are specially brewed at gravities of 5-6% ABV for the Belgian market. Because of the Low Countries traditional trading links with Scotland which pre-date the Union of 1707, Scotch Ale has also long been popular in Belgium. This is a dark sweet strong ale of a type rarely seen in Scotland itself nowadays, most akin to a Wee Heavy. Some British brewery companies actually own breweries in Belgium, such as Whitbread, whilst others have strong connections with Belgium brewing companies which are licensed to brew or factor British products.

It is a measure of the respect in which the Belgian beer market is held that the special high-gravity beers which are produced in Britain for Belgium are usually exclusive to this market, and theses beers are not available on the domestic British market.

Mediæval Belgian brewery

Refreshes the parts other beers cannot reach.
  - Ascribed to Terry Lovelock of Collett, Dickinson, Pearce and Partners for Heineken, 1978.

The Bear, Sandbach

ON THIS DAY IN DECEMBER...

31st December 1935
- During the month of December 135,744 bulk barrels of beer worth £436,971 are imported to the United Kingdom from the Irish Free State, constituting over 96% of all beer imported into the country.

31st December 1963
- Brewing ceases at Candleriggs Brewery, Alloa (George Younger).

SOME CELEBRATORY SONGS

A CHRISTMAS SONG

A Christmas song from the 15th century shows great appreciation for the ale of the time although the quality of the food may leave much to be desired. The sentiment might also be an answer to those who nostalgically call for a return to the Christmas of days gone by:-

(Chorus)
Bring us home good ale, Sir, bring us home good ale,
And for our dear lady, lady love, bring us some good ale.

Bring us home no beef, Sir, for that is full of bones,
But bring home good ale enough, for that my love alone is;
Bring us home no wheaten bread, for it be full of bran,
Neither of no rye bread, for it is of the same:

Bring us home no pork, Sir, for it is very fat,
Neither no barley bread, for neither love I that;
Bring us home no mutton, for that is tough and lean,
Neither no tripes, for they be seldom clean:

Bring us home no veal, Sir, that I do not desire,
But bring us home good ale enough to drink by ye fire;
Bring us home no cider, nor no paled wine,
For if you do thou shalt have Christ's curse and mine.

Say, for what were hopyards meant,
Or why was Burton built on Trent?
Oh many a peer of England brews
Livelier liquor than the Muse,
and malt does more than Milton can
To justify God's ways to man
Ale, man, ale's the stuff to drink
For fellows whom it hurts to think.
    - A. E. Houseman, *A Shropshire Lad.*

He that buys land buys many stones,
He that buys flesh buys many bones,
He that buys eggs buys many shells,
He that buys good ale buys nothing else.
    - John Ray, 1627-1705, *English Proverbs.*

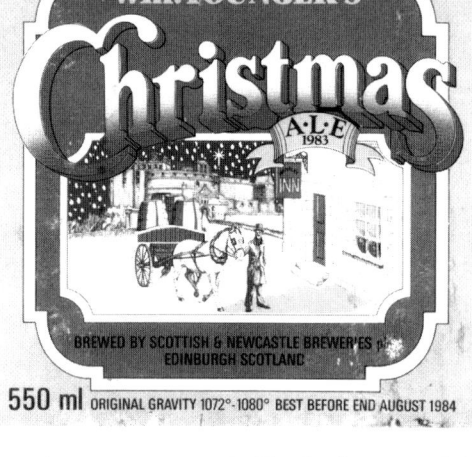

INDEX

A

A Practical Treatise on Brewing   11
Ale
   boiled   13
Ale draper   33
Ale Pole   55
Ale Stake   55
Ale Syllabub   13
Ale-Conner, The   73
Ale-taster   15, 104
Alehouse, The   15, 17, 55
Alehouse-keeper   33
Alehouses   53, 61
Alexander 1st of Scotland   31
Allsopp, Samuel   102
Amenity Ships   111
Anchor Brewery, The   20
Applebie's Journal   92
Assize of Ale, The   73

B

Barclay, Robert   20, 86
Barham, Richard Harris   45
Bass, Michael Thomas   46
Bass Museum and Heritage Centre,
   The   79
Bass, William   47
Beamish   25
Bear Gates, The   31
Beer   8, 28, 65
   bottled   73
   bottom-fermented   121
   brewing of   49
   British   9
   canned   117, 119
   carbonated   65
   definition of   8
   excessive drinking of   49
   haze   9
   hop-based   107
   keg   27, 65, 67, 69
   pasteurised   67
   potable   33
   Pure Laws   8
   quality of   9
   range of   9
   revenue collection of   8
   stout   34, 37, 68, 110
   styles   9
   top-fermented   121
   traditional cask   69
   transport of   89
Beer Act of 1830, The   17
Beer House Act, The   74
Beer House Amendment Act, The   80
Beer of the Empire, The   21
Beer Street   17
Beer-flip   13
Belgian beers   121
Bell, Bartholomew   19, 94
Bell's Beer   19
Black Cork   19
Black, William   11
Bonner, Edward   75
"Bonnie Prince Charlie"   31
Boozer   33
Botham, Ian   57
Breweries
   Adlams   111
   Allsopp   47
   Arrols   113
   Bass   41, 47, 49, 79, 89
   Burton   21, 52, 56, 77, 79, 87
   Calder   93
   Campbells   77
   Candleriggs   103
   Carlsberg   37
   Drybroughs   77
   Eadie   47
   Everard   47
   Flowers   29
   Fowlers   93
   Greens   29
   Holyrood   44
   Jas. Deuchars of Montrose   93
   Marston   47
   Meux   11, 34
   Salt   47
   Scottish and Newcastle   103
   Showells   113
   St. Ann's   32
   Strettons   113
   Tennents   41, 52
   Traquair House   31
   Truman's   18
   Vaux of Sunderland   93
   Whitbread   16, 26, 64
   Youngers   77
Brewers' Journal, The   84
Brewers' yeast   22
Brewing and Distillation   *19*
British Pub, The   61

INDEX

Brodie, William   19
Burton   108, 125
Burton-on-Trent   47

C

CAMRA   69
Carlyle, Thomas   99
Cellarer   47
Chancellor of the Exchequer, The   28
"Charmed Circle, The"   77
Chaucer, William   55
Chettle, Henry   33
Chiswell Street Brewery   16, 54
Churchill, Winston   111
Commissioners of Excise, The   28
Coopers Company, The   40
Coverley, Sir Roger de   52
Customs & Excise Act, 1952   8

D

Defence of the Realm Act, The   25, 81
Delafield, Joseph   20
Dixon, Bernard   27
Double Diamond   69
Dr. Jekyll and Mr. Hyde   19
Duddingston New Brewery   94

E

Edinburgh   10, 77, 79, 87, 95, 97, 99, 103, 107
Edinburgh Society, The   19, 94
Edinburgh-Dalkeith Railway, The   89
Egypt Exploration Society, The   23
Elliot, Thomas   48
Excise office for Scotland, The   19
Export beers   21

F

Farquhar, George   43
Felinfoel Brewing Company, The   117
Fielding, Henry   17
"Fire Mills"   86
First World War, The   11, 25, 41, 74, 81, 85
Foreign malting barley   67
Forth and Clyde Canal, The   87
Fountain Brewery, The   95
Franklin, Benjamin   15
Fuller, Thomas   75

G

George III   54

George, Lloyd   81
Gin Act, The   98
Gin Lane   17
Gladstone, William   101
Grand Trunk Canal, The   56
Guinness   11, 25, 89
Guinness, Arthur   34

H

H.M.S. Menestheus   24, 96
Handsel Monday   10
Harwood, Ralph   11
Heather Ale   107
Herrick, Robert   13
HMS Agamemnon   111
Hodgson, Richard   21
Hogarth, William   17
Hop-searchers   92

I

Incorporation of Wrights, The   19
India Pale Ale   21
Ingoldsby Legends   45
Inns   53
Intoxicating Liquor Act, The   76
Ireland   11, 20, 25, 43, 56, 74, 107, 114
Irish Stout brewers   112

J

Johnson, Dr.   56

K

Keg Investments Ltd.   29
Kind Harts Dreame   33
Kreuger Brewing Co   14

L

Lager   9, 37, 41, 42
  lager louts   49
Lamb's Wool   13, 110
Lay of St. Dunstan   45
Le May, General   27
"Leann Fraoch"   107
Licensing Act, The   84
Licensing hours   17, 81
Long Life   69

M

Malting   8
  process   8
  techniques   8

Mary, Queen of Scots   47
Masters of the Brewers' Company, The   76
Maxwell-Fyfe, Sir David   85
McEwan Hall, The   99
McEwan, William   48, 95
McNeill, Marian   109
Moore, Sir George   108
Morning Chronicle   33
Mother Louse   55
Mother's ruin   17
Murphys   25

N

"Newcastle Beer, The"   16
Newcastle Breweries   57
Newell, Alexander   75
Niall of the Nine Hostages   107

O

Off licences   17
Oxford University   15

P

Pasteur, Louis   88, 122
Pattisons Ltd   12
Pattisons, The   35
Pepys, Samuel   12, 42, 48, 54, 62, 96, 100, 110
Peter the Lay-Brother   45
Porter   9, 11, 20, 21, 25, 34, 87
"Prince of Wales, The"   110
Prohibition   102
Public houses   53

R

Ramsden & Sons, Thomas   14
Ramsden, Captain George   14
Real ale   29
Red Barrel   69
Red Triangle, The   49
Redmond, John   25
Reinheitsgebot   8
Royal Commission on the Sale and Supply of Intoxicating Liquors   40

S

S.S. Egholm   20
Salisbury, Lord   66
Scotch Ale   19
Scott, Sir Walter   99
Scottish and Newcastle Breweries   23

Scottish Brewers Ltd   105
Second World War, The   9, 21, 27, 41, 65, 67, 85, 87
"Shell Scandal", The   81
Shurle, John   15
Sinclair, Sir John   10
Society of Brewers   77
St. Boniface   43
St. Martin   43
St. Matthew   43
St. Theodotus   43
St. Winifrith   43
Stag Brewery   66
State Management Districts, The   14, 32
Steele, Sir Richard   118
Stevenson, Robert Louis   19
Stout   9, 11, 25
Stuart, Charles Edward   31
Stuart, Peter Maxwell   31

T

Tartan Bitter   69
Taverns   53
Temperance cause, The   81
The Beaux Strategem   43
The London Gazette   18
The Times   34
Thrale and Company   40
Thrale's Brewery   56
Traquair House   31
Trent and Mersey Canal, The   87

U

U.S.A.A.F., The   27

W

Wassail   13
Watney's Red   69
Watt, James   16
Watton, Sir Henry   115
Whitbread Tankard   69
Whittington, Dick   76
Williams, Bruce   107
Wine and Beer House Act, The   46

Y

Younger & Co., William   37
Younger, George   105
Younger, William   103